Routledge Revivals

Distributive Trading

First published in 1949, *Distributive Trading: An Economic Analysis* by Margaret Hall offers a detailed examination of the economic dynamics of retail and wholesale trade. Based on rigorous analysis, the book explores topics such as the mounting costs of distribution, advertising, resale price maintenance, and the impact of war on trade. With its in-depth insights into retail and wholesale practices, this work remains a significant resource for understanding the complexities of distributive trade and its economic implications.

Distributive Trading

An Economic Analysis

Margaret Hall

Routledge
Taylor & Francis Group

First published in 1949
by Hutchinson's University Library

This edition first published in 2026 by Routledge
4 Park Square, Milton Park, Abingdon, Oxon, OX14 4RN

and by Routledge
605 Third Avenue, New York, NY 10158

Routledge is an imprint of the Taylor & Francis Group, an informa business

Publisher's Note
The publisher has gone to great lengths to ensure the quality of this reprint but points out that some imperfections in the original copies may be apparent.

Disclaimer
The publisher has made every effort to trace copyright holders and welcomes correspondence from those they have been unable to contact.

For Product Safety Concerns and Information please contact our EU representative GPSR@taylorandfrancis.com. Taylor & Francis Verlag GmbH, Kaufingerstraße 24, 80331 München, Germany

A Library of Congress record exists under LCCN: 50003317

ISBN: 978-1-041-37940-9 (hbk)
ISBN: 978-1-042-01064-6 (ebk)
ISBN: 978-1-041-37941-6 (pbk)

Book DOI 10.4324/9781042010646

DISTRIBUTIVE TRADING
AN ECONOMIC ANALYSIS

by

MARGARET HALL, M.A.

FELLOW OF
SOMERVILLE COLLEGE, OXFORD

HUTCHINSON'S UNIVERSITY LIBRARY
11 Stratford Place, London, W.1
New York *Melbourne* *Sydney* *Cape Town*

THIS VOLUME IS NUMBER 42 IN
HUTCHINSON'S UNIVERSITY LIBRARY

Printed in Great Britain by
William Brendon and Son, Ltd.
The Mayflower Press (late of Plymouth)
at Bushey Mill Lane,
Watford, Herts.

CONTENTS

INTRODUCTION

DISTRIBUTION is the nation's largest industry and it is the one about which we know least. Yet the economics of the distributive trades demand the immediate attention not only of the pure and applied economist but also of every elector in a country where "the Government have accepted as one of their primary aims and responsibilities the maintenance of a high and stable level of employment" and "securing a balanced distribution of industry and labour."[1]

The distributive trades offer the theoretical economist a perfect laboratory for research into the analysis of imperfect competition and oligopoly.[2] They offer the applied economist a theatre of activity hitherto unoccupied, one in which the drama of events is outstanding and the opportunity of revolutionary improvement in the standard of national comfort is not excluded. They offer all of us the challenge of an unsolved problem. The widespread opinion is that all is not well with the distributive trades. Shopping has become one of the most time-consuming and distasteful occupations. To attribute this state of affairs entirely or largely to postwar shortages is, as the subsequent chapters will testify, a form of national self-deception.

It is the aim of this book to provide the reader with the minimum theoretical apparatus and the maximum of available data to enable him to take his own decision on an issue which will become more and not less controversial, more and not less urgent in the United Kingdom as time goes on.

My thanks are due to my husband who has read and criticized the book at every stage and has made an indispensable contribution to Chapters III and IV.

[1]Cmd. 6527 (May, 1944), *Employment Policy*, 3.
[2]See below, 17ff.

THE ECONOMICS OF DISTRIBUTION

CHAPTER I

THE BACKGROUND

National and individual economic problems are compared

SIX years of total war, following what amounted to twenty-one years of more or less desultory economic warfare, both in the domestic and the foreign fields, in the form of cut-throat competition, tariffs and quotas and competitive exchange depreciation, have served to familiarize the individual citizen with the existence of national economic problems. Formerly, so long as the economic activities of government were quantitatively negligible, he thought of economics in terms of earning and spending his own income. Part, indeed, of his income was taken in taxes to finance government expenditure on social services. Certain ways of spending his money were prohibited by law on social grounds. But so extensively was the economic problem an individual one, that the realm of economics was deemed appropriately separate from the realm of politics, and politics alone was conceived as being principally concerned with the aggregate benefit of the community while the scope of economics was virtually restricted to the production and consumption activities of the individual.[1]

While each individual habitually keeps accounts, that is to say, a personal balance sheet of income and expenditure, no such accounts were kept for the nation as a whole until the

[1]Marshall opens his famous *Principles of Economics* 8 (1920), with the following definition: "Political Economy or Economics is a study of mankind in the ordinary business of life, it examines that part of individual and social action which is most closely connected with the attainment and with the use of the material requisites of wellbeing." (Book I, Chapter I, 1.) In the 19th century government expenditure except in wartime, was, quantitatively, sufficiently insignificant to permit the general abandonment of the term and concept of "Political" Economy prior to the Great Depression, 1929-31.

recent war. Annual financial statements of central government revenue and expenditure were, of course, published. But these were balance sheets which necessarily balanced and were unrelated, as far as the ordinary citizen was concerned, to the pattern of production (earning) and consumption (spending) for the nation as a whole; they were not calculated to show the ordinary man what he required to know from his personal accounts, namely, the facts of his economic situation: whether he was living beyond his income, whether he was spending too much on one commodity, e.g. cigarettes, and too little on another, e.g. the education of his children.

During the inter-war period, bitter experience taught us that individual economic activity, with its multiplicity of individual objectives, was influenced to an important extent by factors outside of the individual's control, for example, foreign economic affairs and monetary policy. Such factors, if they were to be regulated at all, must be regulated by the Government on behalf of all the people. This persuasion progressively gained ground in the inter-war period. The 1929-31 world slump hastened the advent of government responsibility for the economic health of the country.

Experience during the inter-war period, the shocking waste occasioned by the unemployment of a minimum of ten per cent of the insured population[1] and by the continual growth of monopolistic practices in trade and industry[2] provided what proved to be irresistible grounds for state intervention to prevent waste. Politicians felt the echo of Marxist theory that capitalism carried within itself the seeds of its own destruction and people wondered whether perhaps these fruits were in fact the chronic unemployment and the steady growth of monopolistic practices, not only in the field of industry but also of trade, which grew from the profit motive. Welfare economics pointed to the means (by state intervention) of maintaining the virtues of capitalism while preventing its vices.

An enormous apparatus, government owned or inspired, of

[1]Between 1921 and 1939, unemployment, among persons insured against unemployment, varied between one and three millions. See Cmd. 6527 (1944), Employment Policy, 6.

[2]See Levy, *The New Industrial System* (1936); id., *Retail Trade Associations* (1942); Burns, *The Decline of Competition* (1936), (U.S.).

social services and regulated sales was accordingly built up in Britain in the nineteen thirties. After the outbreak of war in 1939, emergency[1] powers were taken by the government and consumer rationing, allocation of materials and direction of labour and industry were added to the list.

We live on what we earn

We have now forgotten the dramatic demonstration war provided of the fact that we live, not only as individuals, but as a nation by and on what we earn or produce. The aim of the apparatus of government controls is now to provide a minimum of income and opportunity for all: work for all; food for all; health for all. We, as a nation constitute not only the aggregate of consumers but also the aggregate of producers.

In spite of political dialectic, it is apparent that a high degree of government control of the economic life of the country is no longer, in Britain, an open political issue just because it is no longer optional from the economic point of view. It is all the more urgent that there should be facts and a policy behind the planning and control. Important conditions of successful policy-making and planning are, first, to know the facts; secondly, to interpret them correctly.

The statistical blackout

On the first point; before 1942, when the Government's Central Statistical Office was set up, we were, outside of the fields of employment and of foreign trade, to all intents and purposes, a nation without vital official statistics. The Bank of England published certain statistical series on a monthly basis and its *Monthly Statistical Summary* provided the most comprehensive quantitative data that there were available on the country's economic affairs. A glance at it will show how exiguous was the available statistical material. So, we had governments planning without facts. How can a man plan his expenditure without knowing his income and preferably also something about his previous purchases?

[1]Defence Regulations issued under the Emergency Powers (Defence) Acts, 1939 and 1940, gave the government complete powers to control private property and labour.

In 1941, the first official estimates of national income, in the sense of the aggregate earnings of all members of the community, and of national expenditure, the aggregate expenditure of all members of the community, in the United Kingdom were published[1] and they have been published annually since. Each year improvements are made; but these accounts are still not in a shape which can legitimately be used for planning public policy. Particularly is this true of the field of distribution. Stone, the leading authority on social accounting in this country, writes: "It is hardly possible to use the social account as constructed, in practice, for deciding on the optimum allocation of resources in the same way that private accounts are used for this purpose. The reason is that the social accounts, as at present constructed, like the private accounts, reflect principally private costs and benefits and do not show the community's costs and benefits involved in different courses of action."[2] It should be added that they contain serious gaps: the statistical lights are going on, one by one, but certain parts of the economy and most important, the huge and supremely important field of the distributive trades are still obscure.

No accurate measurement of what the nation spends on distribution is in these circumstances possible. Yet some working estimate must be made. The "real" economic problem, both for the individual and for the nation as a whole, as represented by its government, is how to distribute scarce resources; how to distribute our time and energy, capital and land to earn the maximum "real" income.

Real and money costs

Here we are making a distinction between "real" and "money" cost and between "real" and "money" value. Money is a unit of measurement of economic values just as the yard is a unit of measurement of distance. The money cost of anything is thus the number of units of money required to purchase

[1]Official estimates of national income and expenditure have appeared in the United States since the great depression in 1931 and are published in the *Survey of Current Business* issued by the Department of Commerce. See Stone, *Economic Journal* (September, 1947). "The Measurement of National Income and Expenditure: A Review of the Official Estimates of Five Countries."

[2]Stone, id., 274.

it. What is the "real" cost of anything? The idea of "real" cost relates directly to the economic problem of scarcity. The crux of that problem is that if an "economic", that is a scarce good, is used one way it cannot simultaneously be used another way. Thus, if the individual spends more of his time gardening he has less time to read, or if he spends more of his money income than he did on cigarettes, he will be compelled, unless he can increase his income, to spend less on something else, for example, on the education of his children. The "real", that is, non-monetary cost, consists of the necessity resultant on a given act of consumption of foregoing alternative forms of consumption. From the point of view of the nation, its total real income is the total of goods and services consumed during a given period and the real cost of one act of consumption is the extent to which the community has therefore to forego alternative consumption. Thus, if the community as a whole decides to raise the school-leaving age to fifteen years, the real cost of that desirable purchase is the aggregate of the various economic goods of which it is deprived by that act: namely, the consumer goods that would have been produced by 390,000 children (the number prevented from entering the labour market by raising the leaving age) plus the number of teachers who will have to be added to the teaching force to teach the increased number of pupils, plus the extra houseroom required by school-buildings plus a number of reams of paper and so on.

Can we afford the sum we spend on distribution?

The crucial issues with regard to distribution, which are of course linked, are first, at a time of acute labour shortage, can Britain afford to employ over two and three-quarter million persons (16 per cent of the working population)[1] in the distributive trades as we did before the war; secondly, are we getting our money's worth from that expenditure, that is, are the distributive trades efficient?

On June 12, 1945, the government appointed a Committee "to consider whether, having regard to the importance of information being made available regarding the wholesale or

[1]In June, 1939, 2,887,000 persons were employed in the distributive trades out of a total of 18,000,000 in civil employment. Central Statistical Office, *Monthly Statistical Bulletin* (Feb., 1949.)

retail distribution of goods, a regular Census of Distribution should be instituted. . . ."[1] This Committee reported in favour of closing the widest gap existing in the general statistics of industry. At the present time there are no official data as to the number of traders operating in each type of distributive business nor the total sales of each group. Data there are, but they are not official and they have been collected piecemeal; they do not cover the whole country nor are they strictly comparable. "Without a census, sample cross-sections do not bear a known relation to total trade."[2] The Population Census, last taken in 1931, provides useful data, the relevant substance of which is incorporated in the present volume. This information is now old and it is, anyhow, as it were, a by-product of a census which was undertaken for a different purpose. Even before the war, more than half the total employed workers in the country (of which the distributive and service trades and transport accounted for the major part) were engaged in trades and occupations outside of the main field of productive activity, and for this field the census does not provide a distinct occupational pattern.

Information, both quantitative and descriptive, is, however, available for the United States. Official Census figures are available for 1929, 1935 and 1939 and the data presented are comprehensive. In addition, two government agencies, namely, the Temporary National Economic Committee, appointed in 1938 by President Roosevelt, to investigate and report on the Concentration of Economic Power, and the Federal Trade Commission have published reports on all outstanding aspects of the distribution problem. In spite of the obvious differences in economic conditions in the two countries, of which the most outstanding are the vaster distances which separate producers from consumers in the United States, the greater variation in consumption habits in various regions within the United States, the vaster internal market and the more intensive use of high pressure salesmanship,[3] these American data illustrate many of our own dilemmas.

[1]Cmd, 6764 (1946), *Report of Census of Distribution Committee.*

[2]id., 4.

[3]Federal Trade Commission, *Report on Distribution Methods and Costs* (1944), (U.S.).

The Census of Distribution

On 2nd January, 1947, the President of the Board of Trade (Sir S. Cripps), moving the second reading of the Statistics of Trade Bill providing for a census of production on an annual basis and for a census of distribution, said that the distributive trades were a branch of activity which before the war absorbed the labour of over 2,750,000 people, yet little was known about distribution. He was aware that certain elements in the distributive trades were not anxious to be burdened with this obligation. . . . On the other hand, whenever questions arose, as they constantly did, the first difficulty was lack of any factual data upon which decisions could be reached. What the Government wanted were the facts about distribution. This was not a deep and dark plan preparing for the nationalization of the retail trade . . . they had no intention whatever of nationalizing the distributive trade. . . .[1] A pilot census of distribution has already been begun, relying on voluntary arrangements for the collection of statistics, to guide the government in the best means of making the complete census.

In March, 1947, however, the Government announced the postponement of the full Census of Distribution until 1949. The fuel crisis was given as the occasion for postponement. As the analysis of census data takes a considerable time, the results would not become available until well into the 1950s. Early in 1949, a further postponement was suggested.

Meanwhile, the lack of reliable information on which to base policy does not mean that policy is not being made. In default of any clear picture of what constitutes distribution and the complex of economic issues involved, the distributive trades, in this country, have become the residual legatee of a number of controls vitally affecting their interests but imposed for other purposes: such are consumer rationing and price control; licensing of the sale of food; town planning and a number of others. The daily administration of these controls has affected and continues to affect the issues considered in these chapters: the size of the distributive trades, their organization and the money and real cost of their services which are ultimately met by the shopper.

[1] *The Times* (January 22, 1947).

CHAPTER II

THE MOUNTING COST OF DISTRIBUTION

THE crucial issues with which we are concerned are, first, how much we as a nation can afford to spend on distribution and secondly, whether we are getting our money's worth from our expenditure. The first is the problem of what proportion of the nation's resources of labour and capital, land and enterprise, we are prepared to devote to the provision of distributive services. The second is the problem of the most efficient application of these resources within the industry.

Definition of distribution and of the distributive trades

Distribution is the means by which consumption goods are bought and sold, the process by which output is transferred from the producer to the final consumer. The distributive trades are the aggregate of retail and wholesale outlets engaged in this process. It will be seen that the performance of distributive functions is not restricted to the distributive trades. There is, for instance, a developing tendency for manufacturers themselves to enter the field of distribution by undertaking the wholesale and even retail distribution of their products. Distributive functions are still, however, largely performed by separate distributive trades.

Divorce of production and consumption activities underlies distribution.

We are all consumers and producers but we rarely consume our own products. According to the principle of the division of labour, men earn their incomes by producing a given type of product and spend them on the output of others. This principle has received extended application in the last two centuries and has occasioned remarkable increases in the standard of living. It provides the opportunity for the cultivation of particular productive skills. Most important, it facilitates the manufacture of machinery itself which would be impossible if everyone were compelled to live on his own output. But, as Adam Smith[1] said, the division of labour is limited by the extent of the market. The use of machinery in production allows an increasingly large quantity of goods and services to be made at diminishing cost per unit. This is the basis of large-scale industry. Unless the larger quantities of goods can be marketed it will not be worth while to invest capital in machinery. Thus, it will not pay to introduce machine methods, unless the reduction in cost of production will be greater than the increased cost of reaching additional markets for the larger output. The growth of markets has resulted from two important developments, first, the invention of money and, secondly, the growth of the distributive trades It is not too much to say that without distribution, the fruits of the Industrial Revolution could not have been reaped.

Industrialization has led to the concentration of production of a given type in a given area.[2] Geographical factors like the presence of concentrations of raw materials, nearness to sea-ports, availability of experienced labour underlie this tendency. Whereas we normally concentrate on a narrow range of productive activities, and earn our living in one job, we consume, on the other hand, a great variety of goods and services. The geographical concentration of production of a given type in a given area has given rise to no corresponding geographical pattern of consumption. It is the job of distribution to bridge the gap between producer and consumer. Bridging this gap involves, as will be shown in the following chapters, far more than the coverage of geographical distance. Yet the physical separation of producer and consumer underlies distribution because it occasions the many additional types of market imperfection[3] characteristic of distributive markets.

[1]Smith, *The Wealth of Nations*, 1776, Book I, Chapter 3, Title.

[2]The growth of great urban industrial centres had proceeded so far that the Barlow Committee reported in 1939 (Cmd. 6153, Royal Commission on the Distribution of the Industrial Population) that approximately two-fifths of the total population of the United Kingdom dwelt in seven large towns of more than one million persons. (The corresponding proportion for the United States was stated to be one-fifth.) With the exception of London and Birmingham areas, all the large population groups were dependent on one or two of the basic industries.

[3]cf. 34ff. below for a definition of the term "market imperfection."

Size of the distributive trades

How much is the nation spending on distribution? How big are the distributive trades?

Measuring the size of a given industry is not easy. We can easily measure distances because we know what we mean by the measuring unit, in England, the yard. There is no one obvious unit of measurement for the size of an industry but a variety of units: capital invested; value or volume of turnover; employment, or size of floor space covered.[1] While each of these units provides an indicative measure each gives a different answer to vital questions concerning the growth of a given industry, such as the relative size of an industry at different times and the relative sizes of different industries. There is, over and above these general difficulties, a particular difficulty in measuring an industry as amorphous and heterogeneous as distribution: both a practical problem resulting from the absence of census data and a problem of defining the actual aggregate of firms comprising the industry.

A crude estimate of variations in the size of the distributive trades between the two wars can be obtained, however, by examining changes in (*a*) employment in the distributive trades and (*b*) the value of goods sold at retail. Neither of these measures is, by itself, an accurate measure of changes in the real cost of distribution. Changes in the proportion of labour to other factors of production[2] employed in distribution would impair the reliability of the former measure, while variations in the general level of prices, of which we have no accurate measure for this period in the United Kingdom, anyhow, would affect the index of sales value without affecting, in any important sense, the size of the output of the distributive trades. They are nevertheless capable of showing large-scale movements.

Employment in distribution

It cannot be doubted that a rapid expansion of these trades

[1]This measure was used in connection with the contraction of industry secured under the wartime Concentration of Production Programme.

[2]For example, the introduction of labour-saving devices might lead to a reduction in the numbers employed in distribution but the real cost of distribution would include the labour and other resources employed on the production and maintenance of the labour-saving machinery.

took place in the United Kingdom between the two wars. Using the index of employment as a guide, let us investigate the latest data provided by the Census of Population. They relate to 1931.

The census is computed on the assumption that mankind, in its working capacity, may be grouped for statistical purposes according to two classifications (1) occupational and (2) industrial. The first distinction relates to the kind of work a person does; the second is determined by reference to the business for which a person works. Thus a single business will employ a number of individuals of widely varying occupations for the purpose of creating a particular product.

What is the product of the distributive trades? It is the business of buying and selling. The main business of buying and selling is—

(*a*) the holding of stocks and the supply of credit facilities.

(*b*) the assortment of commodities to be sold into marketable sizes and shapes.

(*c*) the spreading of information.

and (*d*) the carriage of the commodities to be sold from the producer to the consumer.

We can obtain specimen quantitative data[1] relating to the performance of these functions. Corresponding to our first type of function, we find the categories "warehousemen, storekeepers and packers" who numbered (for Great Britain) 243,448 in 1921 and 278,032 in 1931. There is a further category "Persons employed in Finance and Insurance" who numbered 105,515 in 1921 and 137,492 in 1931. The functions listed in the last category are, however, by no means limited to the distributive trades as defined above. Categories (*b*) and (*c*) cannot specifically be related to any of the occupational groups in the census. Our category (*d*) is included somewhere in the following groups "Railway Transport Workers, Road Transport Workers, Water Transport Workers" and "other workers in Transport and Communication." It is impossible here to distinguish between those employed in the transportation of goods from those employed in the transportation of passengers. Even if we could do this, it would still be impossible to distinguish those

[1]Cmd. 6232. *Statistical Abstract of the United Kingdom*, 126, Table 122.

persons whose travel was necessitated by the performance of distributive functions. Wherever common sense presumes that the greater proportion of persons exercising a given function are outside of the distributive trades, we can make no useful deduction from changes in those totals about changes in the total size of the distributive trades. But where the vast majority of persons performing a given economic function are performing that function within the distributive trades, changes in their total numbers over a given period implies a change, in a corresponding direction, in employment in the distributive trades. Such is the category "Commercial Occupations" which is subdivided into "Proprietors and Managers of Wholesale and Retail Businesses" and "Salesmen and Shop Assistants." The former group totalled 463,997 in 1921 and 543,261 in 1931. The latter totalled 352,108 in 1921 and 510,764 in 1931, showing a growth of 17 per cent in the first category and of 45 per cent in the latter during the decade 1921-1931. Bearing in mind that these figures are only illustrative and not comprehensive, we can deduce a general tendency towards expansion in the distributive trades during that decade and also, in view of the far greater percentage increase in the "salesmen and shop assistants" group, we can notice in passing that the average size of distributive units probably increased during this period. In Chapter IV it will be shown that the average size of firm increased as a result of an increase in the proportion of large-scale selling organizations as compared with small-scale unit-shops, rather than because of a general tendency for distributive units to increase in size.

Mounting total of distribution

Such references as the above illustrate the difficulties of quantitative analysis of distribution problems. The Ministry of Labour has, however, published an index of employment[1] in the distributive trades which confirms our conclusions. The official index shows that the numbers in the Distributive Trades

[1]Source: *Ministry of Labour Gazette* (December, 1933), 458f. (1924-1933 inclusive) and *Ministry of Labour Gazette* (January, 1940), 26f. (1934-1939) inclusive. Although there was a change in the basis of the count in June 1927, and workers over 64 were thereafter excluded, the items in the series are stated to be comparable.

rose from 100 in 1923 to 165·6 in 1939 and that every year, except 1935, showed a rise on the previous year. During the same period the total employed in All Industries and Services rose from 100 in 1923 to 128.1 in 1939. Thus, the *proportion* of workers employed in distribution increased during this period.

TABLE I[1]

United Kingdom: Numbers employed in Distributive Trades. 1923-39.

	All Industries and Services. No. of Insured Persons in employment at June	Distributive Trades No. of Insured Persons in Employment at June	Total Insured Workers Index No. June 1923 =100	Employed in Distribution Index No. June 1923 =100
1923	10,188,101	1,180,548	100	100
1924			103·8	108·2
1925			102·9	116·9
1926			—	—
1927	11,061,614	1,509,307	108·6	127·9
1928			107·2	132·2
1929			110·5	136·9
1930			106·1	140·0
1931			101·7	144·3
1932			100·7	149·0
1933			105	152·5
1934			109·5	155·4
1935			111·7	155·3
1936			117·6	160·5
1937			124·6	163·7
1938			121·5	164·5
1939	12,952,769	1,923,843	128·1	165.6

Source: *Ministry of Labour Gazette*, December, 1933, and January, 1940.

[1]It will be noted that these figures do not include small shopkeepers but only *employees.* It has been argued that the increase in the total number of employees is partly accountable to the mortality of small shopkeepers and that large numbers of former proprietors became employees in larger stores during this period. There is no evidence, however, that the *total* number of small shopkeepers declined during this period, though the mortality of individual small shopkeepers was high. Cf. Smith, *Retail Distribution*[2] (1948), page 86.

No figure for 1926 is published. The general strike occurred in that year.

Measured in terms of employment, then, the distributive trades expanded rapidly between the two wars. The above employment figures represent the use of an increasing proportion of the nation's resources in the field of trade as contrasted with industry until, on the outbreak of war, out of a total industrial population[1] (June, 1939), of 18,000,000, no fewer than 2,887,000, that is sixteen per cent. of the total, were employed in distribution. Thus, distribution was in the United Kingdom on the outbreak of war the largest industry in the country (measured in terms of employment) and it employed more than the total number engaged in primary production (mining and agriculture) namely 1,823,000, and 41 per cent of the numbers employed in secondary production (manufacture) namely, 7,705,000. If we include also the numbers engaged in performing distributive functions, while not being classified as distributive workers, the relationship becomes even more striking.[2]

Comparison with United States

In the United States, also, employment in the distributive trades increased to an appreciable extent during this period. The numbers employed in wholesale distribution increased 5.9 per cent. between the years 1930 and 1940 to a total in 1939 of 1,695,646 persons, of whom 133,698 were active proprietors and 1,561,948 were employees on a salary or wage basis. The percentage increase in population, during this period, was 7.2,

[1]Employment figures taken from the *Monthly Statistical Bulletin*. It will be observed that these figures relate to total industrial population (total number of males aged 16-64 and females aged 14-59, gainfully employed, whether employers, employees or working on their own account) whereas Table I relates to insured persons alone.

[2]An estimate of the total numbers engaged in the provision of distributive services, made on the basis of 1931 census data, gives a total of "well over five million people in Great Britain" occupied in distribution out of a total of twenty-one million. Fabian Publications, Ltd. *Research Series No.* 108. *Distribution: The Case for a National Census*. Report of a Group of Fabians (F. A. Cobb, M.P., Joan Mitchell, Charles Smith, M.P.) based on evidence submitted to a Board of Trade committee on the Census of Distribution, March, 1946.

and the labour force increased from 48,594,592 in 1930 to 52,789,499, a 9 per cent increase.[1] In remarkable contrast to this country, the total number of persons in *full time* employment in *retail* distribution was practically the same in 1939 (5,811,998) as in 1929 (5,721,220), while there was the substantial increase of 56 per cent in the number of part-time employees from 557,074 in 1929 to 869,285 in 1939. In 1939, persons employed in retail and wholesale trade constituted 16 per cent of the working population. Thus, the proportion of full-time employment in the distributive trades *declined* in the pre-war decade in the United States[2] while in this country it appreciably increased.

This remarkable contrast would be easier to explain if it could be shown that the service provided by retailers and wholesalers in this country was superior to that supplied by traders in the United States. This cannot be shown. Moreover, if it is true that the wealthier a community is, the larger proportion of resources it will be desirable for it to devote to tertiary as contrasted with primary and secondary employment, then it is even more surprising that both the proportion of persons employed in distribution pre-war and the growth of that proportion during the inter-war period should be substantially greater in this country than in the U.S.

In the following chapters, explanations are put forward. An attempt is made to identify (*a*) factors making for an excessive increase in the number of trading units and in the services they supplied (size of the distributive trades) and (*b*) factors tending

[1]Persons in the labour force fourteen years and over. *Sixteenth Census of the United States* (1940), Part I, Vol. II, *Population*, 50, Table 20.

[2]It is interesting to note that in the United States the number of retail establishments increased from 1,543,158 in 1929 to 1,770,355 in 1939, an increase of nearly 15 per cent. In the same period the number of wholesale establishments increased from 168,820 to 200,573, an increase of nearly 19 per cent. There are no comparable figures available for England and Wales, but the number of proprietors and managers of retail businesses, which is some indication of the number of shops, rose between the two census years from 352,108 in 1921 to 569,100 in 1931, an increase of over 60 per cent. (The later figure is quoted from the discussion of the size of the retail trade in Smith, *Retail Distribution*, page 35).

These figures have some bearing on the increasing size of the industry in this country, and particularly on our further problem of changes in the size and character of establishments and their relation to the real cost of distribution.

to prevent the adoption of business methods and forms of organization leading to a reduction of average distributive costs (organization of distributive trades). First, however, let us examine the legitimate causes of expansion.

Was the pre-war expansion economic?

What were the reasons for expansion and were they legitimate from the economic point of view, that is, did they correspond to a greater desire or need on the part of the community for distributive services and were the increased resources deployed in the most efficient manner?

Nineteenth century economic theorists would have argued that the very fact that an expansion in the number of persons engaged in trading took place was proof of an increased need for their services. Their argument ran: people conduct industry and trade for private profit. Profits equal receipts minus costs. The receipts of a given form of enterprise increase as a result either of an expansion of business or an increase in charges or prices or both. These contingencies can only arise when the consumers, in the aggregate, have decided to spend more money on the commodity or service in question. They only take this decision when they *want* it more than they did. As will be seen in the following chapters, later theory has exposed two types of fallacy underlying this train of thought. The first is that for reasons like the inequality of personal incomes, it does not necessarily follow that, when the community spends more on a given commodity or service, they want it more in any sense distinct from offering more money for it. This can be illustrated by supposing that a change takes place in income distribution. This will lead to changes in the pattern of expenditure even though the pattern of consumers' preferences remains unchanged. Secondly, the classical presumptions are only plausible in a purely competitive market and to-day imperfections and monopolistic practices are inherent in every sector of the economic life of the community. Later theory, therefore, does not hold that the fact that something happens as a result of the working of the pricing system necessarily raises a presumption that the thing that happens is desirable from the economic point of view. Thus it was not economically desirable that there should have been between one and three million unemployed in this country in the inter-war period. Yet there were. Equally, there is no presumption that the distributive trades should have achieved the most economic size and organization in the inter-war period. We need to determine the causes and results of the expansion before we can determine its legitimacy from the economic standpoint.

We thus proceed to investigate the expansion of the distributive trades relatively to other relevant quantities like population or volume of trade, in order to get the problem into perspective. Legitimate occasions for the employment of increasing numbers in distribution there were, such as increasing population and an increasing volume of goods to be distributed. We have also instanced the greater geographical separation between consumers and producers which attended progressive industrialization and a factor, perhaps still more important during the period we are considering—ribbon development.[1] Others bring forward the wartime (World War I) lag in the provision of new shops[2] as legitimate grounds of expansion between the two wars.

The census of 1921 gave the population of the United Kingdom as 44,027,000. By 1931 the total had increased to 46,038,000 (4 per cent increase) and by 1939 to an estimated 47,762,000 persons (3·7 per cent increase). In comparison, the number of those employed in distribution rose 44.3 per cent between 1923 and 1931 (1921 figure not available), and a further 15 per cent between 1931 and 1939 (Ministry of Labour Index rose from 144.3 in 1931 to 165.6 in 1939).

Ford calculates that the absolute increase in the number of shops does not correspond to an increase in relation either to the total population or to the number of families; on the contrary, he estimates a decrease in the number of shops per 1,000 of population at 0·26 per cent and per 1,000 families at 11·5 per cent. "The census of 1921 gave the number of shops as 615,000, or one per fifteen families. This information was not given in

[1]Levy, *The Shops of Britain* (1947), 2.
[2]Ford, "Excessive Competition in the Retail Trades. Changes in the Number of Shops, 1901-1931," *Economic Journal* (September, 1935), 501ff.

1931, and for this year we have to rely upon the total number of occupied persons who returned themselves as owners or managers of retail businesses. This was 569,000 or one per eighteen families."[1]

It appears then that the numbers employed in distribution rose much more than in proportion to the total population and were an increasing proportion of the industrial population, but that the number of business units increased nothing like so rapidly.

What evidence is there on the volume of goods to be distributed? The only means of computing an aggregate volume of goods is by summing their money value but changes in the price level, that is in the value of money itself, affect this total and appropriate allowances have to be made. The Bank of England Statistical Summary shows that the official index of the money value of retail sales rose from 101 (1933=100) in 1932 to 125 in 1937. Between 1937 and 1939 it rose a further 5 per cent.[2] But prices meanwhile had varied and we have no suitable measure of the variation of prices. The official cost of living index fell from 226 (1914—100) in 1921 to 147.5 in 1931. and rose again to 158 in 1939. This index relates to price movements for a particular class of goods only—those bought by people with working-class incomes.[3] None but the roughest estimate can thus be made of changes in the volume of goods to be sold.[4] Taking all the available evidence into account such an estimate has been made by the group of Fabians referred to

[1]Ford, id., 503f.

[2]cf. *Bank of England Statistical Summary* for average monthly totals on which this index is based.

Note: The base of the official index, published in the *Board of Trade Journal*, was changed in 1937.

[3]Until June 1947, when the basis of the index was revised, the index was based on an examination of working-class expenditure in 1914. (Cmd. 7077 (March, 1947), *Interim Report of the Cost of Living Advisory Committee*.)

[4]The annual value of retail sales 1924-1945 and the annual retail price index moved as follows:

United Kingdom—Value of Retail Sales and Retail Price Index, 1924—1945.

Year	*Estimated Value of Retail Sales* (£m.)	*Retail Price Index*	*Year*	*Estimated Value of Retail Sales* (£m.)	*Retail Price Index*
1924	2,480	100	1929	2,717	94
1925	2,558	100.5	1930	2,788	90
1926	2,559	99	1931	2,499	84
1927	2,585	96	1932	2,298	82
1928	2,636	95	1933	2,098	79

above and they conclude that[1] "during the decade 1927-1937, the goods handled per distribution worker increased by only ½ per cent per annum, compared with an annual increase in production of 2½ per cent in output per production worker." Smith's view is "the rise in the cost of distribution, reflected in the falling volume of sales per worker, continued until 1933 and was followed by a period in which the rising volume of total retail sales moved very closely parallel to the still rising total of distributive employment."[2] There is little to be said for having more people distributing fewer goods.

Such estimates lead to the gloomy conclusion that improvements in the technique of production have not been paralleled in the field of distribution. Lest it should be supposed that technical improvements in distribution of a labour-saving and cost reducing kind are not practicable because the character of trading differs in a fundamental manner from that of production, we have only to cite American experience to the contrary. The U.S. Census of Business estimates that the physical volume of goods sold at retail increased by seven or eight per cent between 1929 and 1939 and that this increase in the volume of work to be done was met entirely by the recruitment of part-time labour.

The Cost of Distribution

The rising trend of resources applied to distribution is paid for by the community in the prices it pays for its shopping. Distributors' margins must cover distributors' costs for profitable business. No official estimate of the overall cost of distribution is available. Smith has computed, in the light of available data, that the total money cost of distribution in 1924 was nearly 23 per cent of the retail values[3] and that the cost of retail distri-

[1]Fabian Publications, Ltd., 1d.,
[2]Smith, *Retail Distribution*,[2] (1948), 144.
[3]Smith, *Retail Distribution*,[2] (1937), 141, Table VI.

Year	*Estimated Value of Retail Sales* (£m.)	*Retail Price Index*	*Year*	*Estimated Value of Retail Sales* (£m.)	*Retail Price Index*
1934	2,151	80	1940	2,994	113
1935	2,282	81	1941	3,080	124
1936	2,413	83	1942	3,297	128
1937	2,623	88	1943	3,263	129
1938	2,681	90	1944	3,470	131
1939	2,740	92	1945	3,631	132

Source: Smith, *Retail Distribution*,[2] (1948) 145, Table VII.

bution constituted 70 per cent of total distribution costs. He estimates, further, that by 1931, the total cost of distribution had risen to nearly 48 per cent of the factory value of retail sales and that, of the total cost of distribution, retail distribution constituted by this time, no less than 78 per cent. In fact, it became an increasingly expensive business!

More recent estimates support these general conclusions. Cadbury[1] stated that under wartime conditions, in the confectionery trade, the cost of retailing and wholesaling amounted to about one-third of the retail price. Cadbury also quotes the Ministry of Food's estimate that the total value of food sales (excluding chocolate confectionery, alcoholic drinks and mineral waters) was about £900 million a year when they entered the chain of distribution in their finished state, and that they were sold for £1,350 million. By far the greater part was the cost of retailing. For articles other than food there is insufficient evidence on which to compute the overall cost of distribution but what is known about particular groups suggests that it may be even greater. It looks as though of every £1 the consumer spends, between 6s. and 10s. and sometimes considerably more goes for distribution.

An estimate made by a group of Fabians for submission to the Census of Distribution Committee[2] puts the cost of distribution even higher: "An unknown part of the price of goods goes to pay for their distribution. The relative division of effort between production and distribution shows that this part must be large. In 1938, £2,801 million was spent on goods, from personal incomes. Probably, over £1,000 million of this was paid for distribution."

A simple check on the order of magnitude of distribution costs can be obtained by reference to war-time experience of government price control. Distribution was of the first order of importance to the civilian front during the war. The government's problem in wartime price control[3] was to determine maximum prices and maximum mark-ups at a level which would cover the costs of distribution of the least efficient distributor which it was desired to keep in production because any

[1]Cadbury Brothers, Ltd., *Industrial Record*, 1919-39, 52.
[2]Fabian Publications, Ltd., id.
[3]The particular problems of distribution in wartime are dealt with below, 171ff.

but a uniform price for each price-controlled commodity was held to be difficult and costly to administer. For utility goods, i.e. standardized non-food consumers' goods (clothing and household goods) the government fixed both a maximum price and a maximum permitted mark-up for all traders. The wholesaler was permitted to add a maximum of 20 per cent of the price at which he bought from the manufacturer and the retailer, a maximum varying between 33⅓ per cent and 43 per cent (for different classes of goods) to the price he paid the wholesaler. In the field of food, the government price ceilings allowed comparable margins. The permitted mark-ups were intended to cover distribution costs. They afford an indication of the addition to the final price which is frequently paid by consumers on account of distribution costs.

The initial reaction to the above statistics showing the order of magnitude of marketing costs and their progressive increase in the inter-war period is to say that marketing methods in this country must be grossly inefficient. Reference is made to the number of retail stores.[1] On the outbreak of war, there were some 750,000 retail shops, possibly more, that is approximately one to every sixty persons in the community or one to every fifteen families. One retail shop can certainly conveniently service more than sixty persons and if it serves only sixty persons, salespeople will be standing idle during much of their working day.

No estimate of the efficiency of the distributive trades can, however, be made except in the light of the organizational pattern of these trades and of the economics of marketing.

A simple criterion of efficiency of the distributive trades in general would be: can the consumer get what he wants, when he wants it, at a price he wants it, with as little call on the scarce resources of the community as possible? But this latter is itself affected by the size of the working population and the amount of capital and land devoted to production. In this respect, therefore, as competitors for scarce national resources, distribution conflicts with maximum production and economic theory must provide the analytical tools whereby we can decide what is the most efficient division of resources between production and distribution.

[1]The Linlithgow and Samuel Commissions criticized the number of shops.

CHAPTER III

ECONOMIC ANALYSIS OF RETAIL TRADE

THE economics of retailing has not been treated completely satisfactorily in general works on economics for reasons which will appear in the course of this chapter.

The method of economics

For teaching and examination purposes at Oxford, economics is usually divided into so-called "theory" and so-called "organization": and, elsewhere, the terms "pure" and "applied" economics are used in much the same sense and for much the same purpose. The former is an attempt to identify, by the methods of economic analysis, cause and effect in the economic world. The second takes the form of a descriptive account of the economic world and is, at its best, a representation of the facts of the case. As a practical teaching matter, it is difficult to determine which of this chicken and egg should come first. This particular chicken-egg dilemma ought not, however, to arise in so far as the progress of economic theory can only be made hand-in-hand with a careful examination of the ever-changing economic organizations which are its subject-matter. Theory which proceeds without constant verification of its hypotheses is a menace. Hypotheses it requires. Economists, denied as they are the method of experimentation, because reality cannot for the purpose of their investigations be segmented and immobilized, must exclude some of the manifold of reality by a process of thought involving the making of assumptions.

Unless they deal with their problems in this selective manner, they are left with the "chaos congenial to the empirical mentality." But there are good and bad assumptions. Those assumptions which exclude what, for a given investigation, are the most important parts of reality are bad and vice versa. To have at hand as comprehensive as possible information on the facts would, therefore, seem to be indispensable to this procedure.

The economic motive

Economic theory sets out to explain how people act in various circumstances, if they are trying to do as well for themselves as possible. In the words of Jevons[1] writing in 1871: "the theory . . . may be described as the mechanics of utility and self-interest." To apply this theory to real life, we have first to identify the actual circumstances, and then to decide whether the people concerned *are* trying to better themselves in the economists' sense of the phrase. In the retail trade, the circumstances are complex and the meaning of improving one's position is difficult to decide.

Applied to retailing

We can begin with the assertion that retailers in Great Britain and in most other countries have to keep solvent and therefore cannot long continue at a loss, and that, in general, they would also prefer to choose the more profitable of alternatives otherwise similar. The condition assumed by economists in general value theory is that each firm will try to make its profits as large as it can. If other firms can enter any trade freely, then there will be movement between trades in such a way that greater competition will reduce large profits and less competition will increase small profits, until each trade is about as profitable as any other, and the general level of profits will be just high enough to keep business men in business but not so high that other workers will want themselves to set up their own firms. This gives the position of perfect competition, where all prices tend to the level which covers costs of efficient operation, including interest on the capital employed, and an adequate return for the trouble of management.

Retailers' costs

If this is applied to retailing, the retailers' costs comprise the prices he pays for his goods, his rent, rates, wages and other running expenses and his own "normal" profits[2] without which

[1]Jevons, *Theory of Political Economy*, 4 (1911), 21.

[2]The trader's gross margin (profit) is the difference between the value of his sales and the cost price of his wares; the trader's net margin (profit) is the difference between his gross margin and his operating costs.

he would not be there. His returns are his receipts from sales. If the difference between his receipts from sales and his costs were higher than the level of profits elsewhere, other people would open shops, and the total effect of their actions would be either to raise costs, including the costs of selling the goods, or to lower selling prices, until it was no longer attractive to enter the occupation. At this point, the consumer would be getting his retail services as cheaply as possible. While this is obviously an heroic oversimplification, it is nevertheless the heart of the matter and a good beginning. The public require to have retail outlets in order to do their shopping conveniently and they have to make it worth while for someone to run the shops; but if it is much more than worth while, new shops are likely to be opened, and there cannot thereafter be as much profit for individuals in the trade as there was before.

When will retailing pay? Some tools of analysis

Underlying this traditional conception of "normal" profits, is the idea of an industry as an aggregate of firms each supplying one and the same product. It is recognized that both the total and average costs of the typical firm will vary with changes in output, showing in general an increase in total costs for all increases in output and a decrease in average cost over certain ranges of output, corresponding to the economies of scale, followed eventually by rising average costs due to the diseconomies of running "over-full". A further derived concept is that of marginal cost; the increase in total cost incurred as a result of producing another unit of output.[1] The individual seller will aim at producing and selling that amount of output for which marginal cost equals marginal revenue because that is his most profitable output. This result follows directly from the defini-

[3]The average cost of producing n units is $\frac{total\ cost}{n}$. The marginal cost of producing the nth unit is the total cost of producing n units minus the total cost of producing (n—1) units. The marginal revenue for the nth unit is the total receipts for selling n units minus the total receipts for selling (n-1) units. When the demand curve is downward sloping, showing that increased quantities must be marketed at lower prices, the computation of marginal revenue will show both a positive quantity (the price of the nth unit) and a negative quantity (the multiple of the price reduction required to market n instead of (n-1) units and the number of units previously sold.)

tion of marginal revenue (or rceeipts) and marginal cost together with the assumption that producers will behave in such a way as to maximize their profits. In the following diagram measuring output along Ox and money, whether cost or price, along Oy, OM is the output for which marginal cost mc= marginal revenue (mr); it (OM) is the most profitable output because if output were increased beyond OM, say to OM_1, the increment to cost on account of the production of MM_1, with marginal cost M_1P_1) would be greater than the increment to receipts for selling MM_1 (M_1R_1). If less than OM were produced, profits could be increased by increasing production so long as the marginal revenue exceeded the marginal cost. In competition,[1] where price is invariable with the output of the particular seller, the position will be as follows:

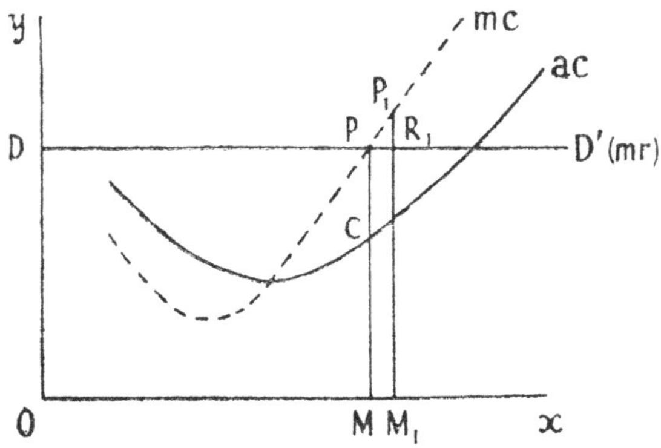

Fig. 1

Equilibrium of the Firm in Perfect Competition

Competitive markets

Where, as in the above case, average receipts MP are greater than average costs MC for the output which the seller decides to market (OM), wherever other firms can enter the industry freely, they will do so, induced by the "abnormally" high rate of profit CP. The influx of new firms will continue,

[1]This analysis follows closely the accepted form as seen in numerous writings, for example, Chamberlin, *Theory of Monopolistic Competition*[3] (1938), 11ff.

unless monopoly or the non-homogeneity of the factors of production prevents some from taking up an equally favourable position with others, until all firms are marginal and only normal profits, just high enough to keep business men in business but not so high that other workers will themselves want to set up their own firms, remain.

Imperfectly competitive or monopolistically competitive markets

The demand curve (DD^1 in Figure I) shows the average price consumers are willing to pay for quantities of output shown on Ox. In competition, where the individual seller's output is a negligible proportion of the whole, this price does not vary with variations in the volume of his sales. In many cases, namely, wherever some element of monopoly is present, this is not the case; the demand curve confronting the individual seller will then be downward sloping (DD^1 in Figure II) and the marginal revenue curve mr will not any longer coincide with the demand curve.

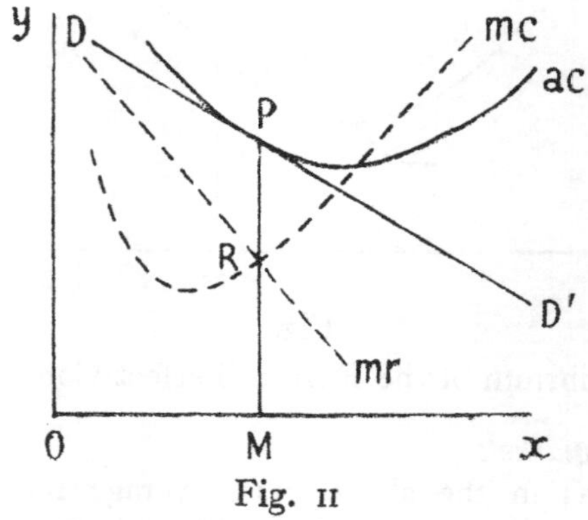

Fig. II

The individual producer will still endeavour to maximize his profits by equating marginal cost with marginal revenue (at MR for the output OM) and the traditional analysis holds, furthermore, that new entrants will equate average receipts with each producer's average costs wherever more than normal profits occur. Both average costs and average receipts are thus shown equal to MP in Figure II. But whether or not that is so, once we assume oligopoly,[1] we certainly cannot assume that the condition of normal profits involves the elimination of all profits above a level which is the supply price of management. We defined normal profits as that level of profits which provides no incentive either to expansion or contraction of the individual price. It seems very doubtful whether the association[2] of the downward sloping demand curve with the assumption of such a complete condition of free entry as to secure the obliteration of abnormal profits is useful. Application of the assumption of oligopoly to these conditions would suggest that something more like the following would prevail. When the individual retailer observes that some retailer or other was receiving more than normal profits, he will take into account the fact that if he sets up in competition, the two of them will have to share the available market. Thus, in the simplest possible case, when the setting up of a new shop would simply lead to each shopkeeper getting half of the total business, which we are assuming, for simplicity, remains unchanged, it would require the receipt by some shopkeeper of twice as great profits as normal to induce a new competitor to set up shop. A modification of the theory of normal profits as the condition of equilibrium in imperfect competition is thus seen to be required so soon as oligopoly is supposed: and oligopoly is inherent in imperfect competition. The theory of normal profits can now be re-stated as follows: Unequal rates of profit as between traders is consistent with group equilibrium, providing any potential entrant to the trade would consider that the fact of his setting up a shop in the area would reduce the rate of profit below the normal level, i.e. the level required to keep him in business.

Peculiar character of the retail market.

The complexities of retailing arise from the following facts.

First: consumers are spread over space and costs of transport either for them to visit the retailer or for the retailer to

[1]See page 41

[2]cf. Chamberlin: *Theory of Monopolistic Competition,*[3] (1938), 74.

deliver the goods (if he does deliver) will be different for each customer and for each shop. Thus, there cannot *in any circumstances* be perfect competition in retail trade; for this to obtain all buyers must be similarly situated in respect of each supplier.

How the retailer can maximize his profits

But shall the economic forces, incentives, arising from causes like the geographical distribution of consumers and the personal tie between shopper and shopkeeper, be represented by a falling demand curve (denoting a degree of monopoly) or a rising cost curve (denoting the necessity for increased expenditure to increase the volume of sales)? The answer is that it is best denoted by the use of both means. Differentiation[1] of the product in retailing arises in a wide variety of ways, all the ways in which a shopkeeper can make his shop more attractive than others. There is a degree of monopoly wherever differentiation of the product arises. The individual distributive trader's demand curve must, accordingly, in every instance be considered downward sloping (as in figure 2). But the fact is that the retailer can increase his sales by extra selling costs which induce people to buy from him *who would not be attracted by any price reduction* because they would not even know of his existence unless some new advertisement, for example, had caught their eye. The fact that increased expenditure on selling costs results in increasing the aggregate of his customers (and thus his total volume of sales), gives rise to increasing marginal costs for increased sales and, when the increase in marginal selling costs is greater than any realized decrease in the burden of overhead costs per unit of sales, average costs also will rise. The retailer has thus a double problem in maximizing his profits: (1) to equate marginal cost with marginal revenue for any given body of customers. This is the business of determining the appropriate price at which to sell. (2) to decide how far to strive to extend his goodwill, that is the total number of his customers. This is a matter of expenditure on selling costs directed primarily not at increasing the purchases of existing customers but at attracting marginal customers.

The two decisions referred to above are not in reality

[1]This important concept is more fully explained below, page 38ff.

successive but simultaneous. The retailer's decision on business policy is thus seen to be the solution of a simultaneous equation. This point is dealt with more fully at a later stage.

Secondly, each retailer handles a variety of different goods, and has to decide the margin or mark-up for each one in the light of his estimate of its probable rate of turnover and of the effects of the price he charges for it on (*a*) the number of purchasers of the commodity in question and (*b*) his "goodwill", that is the aggregate of his customers. These concepts will become plainer when we apply the analysis to the facts of the case. The more lines he carries, the more difficult it is for him to make reasoned estimates for any one of them.

Thirdly, a number of goods, but by no means all, have to be sold at fixed prices set by the manufacturers. Where re-sale price maintenance of this kind is practised, price competition as envisaged by much economic analysis cannot occur at all.

A Departmental Committee was appointed[1] in July 1947 and is still[2] in session, to consider "the practice by which minimum wholesale or retail prices or margins for the resale of goods are fixed by producers and its effects on supply, distribution and consumption and to report whether, in the light of present conditions and particularly of the need for maximum economy and efficiency in the production and distribution of goods, any measures are desirable to prevent or regulate its continuance." The appointment of this commission is evidence of the growing public recognition of the importance of the distributive trades in general and a particular aspect of the economics of distribution-resale price maintenance.

It is a surprising and regrettable fact that the terms of reference of this Committee invite it to consider the problems before it in the light of 1938 conditions. No account is to be taken of the whole of wartime experience and the fundamentally different alignment of economic forces associated with full employment (see Appendix to the present Chapter). This means that the committee's findings will be of historical importance only.

Finally, there is the fact that the retailer, by spending

[1] *Board of Trade Journal* (October 4, 1947.)
[2] (April 1949. It reported in June. Cd. 7696.)

money on advertising, delivery and other services to his customers, can add something to value of the goods he sells which differentiates them not only from the goods of other retailers, but which may also differentiate them in respect of his own customers, since some of them may attach importance to services which add nothing in the eyes of others. There is thus nothing which corresponds exactly to the simple idea of a commodity, which is the basic concept of ordinary economic analysis.

It will be seen, then, that traditional economics, based as it was in Britain prior to the 1930's, on the following assumptions: absence of transport costs; independence of forces operating on the demand side from forces operating on the supply side; perfect knowledge; and a number of indistinguishable units of a homogeneous commodity *excludes* the field of distribution, by hypothesis! These hypotheses are, for the purpose of the economics of distribution, bad hypotheses according to the definition given above.

Retail trade is inherently imperfectly competitive

All the characteristics just described are examples, in one form or another, of the phenomena of market imperfection to which increasing attention has been paid in recent theoretical work, but which certainly cannot be said to have reached any certain or final results. The difficulties arise because the material dealt with has become too complex for the old generalizations. Hence the necessity for rejecting the rigid "theory versus organization" dichotomy. Particularly difficult in these circumstances is the concept of a commodity, referred to in a preceding paragraph. To the economists of the nineteenth century, this was clearly defined as something which was in some sense a physically identifiable entity, the same to everyone. It is interesting to note that, according to Jevons,[1] the word commodity originally meant utility. It is now used as a generic term denoting any economic or scarce good. The producer could turn it out by spending a known amount, and unless there was either a monopoly or a factor of production the units of which were not homogeneous, all efficient producers (and

[1]Jevons, *Theory of Political Economy* (1871), Chapter III.

these were the only ones who could survive) could get similar results by similar expenditure. In the same way, consumers were all supposed to want the same physical object and to be indifferent to the frills: and they were supposed to exist in "markets", in which consumers were also indifferent to where the objects actually were. This made it possible to speak of market demands and market supplies which were conceived as the sum of individual demands and supplies, and it followed that any unit of the supply could meet equally well any unit of the demand. It is the essence of retailing that this is not generally true. (One might also go so far as to question whether it is now any longer widely applicable to production in this country at the present time.) Further, there was a clear distinction between sellers' costs and consumers' bids which followed from the idea of a physical commodity. But when the volume of sales depends partly on the amount of selling costs, it becomes much less easy to distinguish between an increase of costs and a reduction of price. Economics is essentially a study of the relations between supply and demand, and it is, therefore, a primary requisite to be able to distinguish between them, which becomes difficult if, for example, demand increases *because* supply is more expensive.

Clarifications of assumptions

Returning now to expand the central part of the analysis in order to understand the processes at work, we must begin with a simplified assumption. We stand in need of simplifying assumptions but they must be good and serviceable ones in the sense defined above. Let us consider a number of retailers each selling only one commodity, for which they all pay the same price to the manufacturers or wholesalers: and assume that they are free to add as great or as small a mark-up as they choose. Each will then have two methods of attracting customers: by lowering the final price or by adding something to the basic commodity, which he can do, for example, by offering free delivery; by making his shop more attractive, for example, with more space, or rest-rooms, or decorations, or assistants; or, by advertising devices which will persuade the customers that his goods are better than those sold elsewhere. In order to make the problem susceptible of analysis at all, we must assume that it is possible to find out the effects of these various possibilities, that is, that the retailer can judge how much each customer will be affected by each price and by each combination of selling expenses.

Let us first ask what he would do if he tried to fix a price which would make his profits a maximum. In the absence of competition, as he lowers his price, he will be able to sell more of the commodity than before and will gain the proceeds for any article on the additional sales, but will lose the sum of the price reductions on the amount he was selling at the previous price. The difference is called the marginal revenue.[1] The extra cost of the extra goods sold is called the marginal cost, and as long as this is less than the marginal revenue for the sale of any article, it will pay to lower its price and expand sales. When the two are equal, it will not pay to lower prices any more. But at this point, it will pay the retailer to spend more on selling costs and attract extra customers until the net[2] gain from the sales to them (which is *not* accompanied by losses because there is no need either to lower price or to spend in order to attract the customers who were already buying from the retailer) is just balanced by the extra costs.

Selling costs and goodwill

However, the new customers increase his total demand (goodwill) and may therefore cause him to revise his price: but, if he does this, he will find again that a different selling outlay will probably be more profitable. Thus, if the pattern of consumer preferences remained unchanged, and the conditions under which he was incurring his costs remained the same, his most profitable position would be when the marginal revenue from further price reductions equalled the marginal cost for the average customer and when the marginal receipts from additional custom equalled the marginal cost of

[1]cf. page 32 above.

[2]Price minus prime cost. By the term "prime" cost is meant the addition to total cost resulting from the sale of the extra unit the main constituent of which will be the price paid by the retailer, for example, to the wholesaler or manufacturer for the article in question.

further sales expenditure. Thus, he has a double problem: to find the most profitable price at which to sell to his customers, and to find the number of customers to whom it pays him to sell at a given price.

Individuality of consumer preferences

The particular characteristic of retailing is that customers are different from one another, both in their tastes and in their residences: in general, it costs more and more to attract the extra custom because it comes from those who live farther and farther away, or from those who are less and less susceptible to particular selling methods. Thus we would expect the typical retailer to have, as it were, a circle of customers: he makes most profits on those whom he attracts with least selling effort, while those on the fringe are only paying him about as much as it costs him to keep their custom. If we now imagine other retailers entering the field, it will obviously pay them to keep as far as possible out of each other's way, by catering for that part of the trade which has a different taste, or lives out of the range of the existing retailers. This would be the situation, for example, where there was one butcher in each suburb of a town, or several dressmakers in one suburb, each appealing to a different social or income group. They would each be protected from the others, not because they had monopolies in the usual sense of the term, but because it cost each one too much to enter the field of others to make it worth while doing so. Each has some control over the price which he can charge, but this sets the maximum selling outlay which it is worth incurring and therefore the total number of customers that he will attract. As long as it does not pay to break into the neighbouring territories, that is as long as the reduction of overheads is not sufficient to offset the increased costs of extending sales over a wider area, all is well.

Retail market, like all imperfect markets, readily gives rise to conditions of oligopoly

It is inherent in this situation that conditions of oligopoly may arise at any time. By oligopoly is meant a situation in which the seller, in determining his price and output policy, takes into account the probable reactions of his competitors to changes in *his* policy. Thus, if some shopkeepers are now making abnormal profits, that is, if the sum of the profits on each customer comes to be more than enough to make it worth while to enter the business, competition will appear, and there is now no longer room for all the firms to do what pays best without worrying about loss of custom. Each will have some customers who like his methods or live near him, while others will be attracted to the new-comers. At this stage, the problem becomes more difficult: the firm which is losing trade has to decide whether to acquiesce in this, or to compete by price reductions or expansion of selling costs. Whichever course is adopted will mean less profits for him: in the first case, from reduced volume of sales and turnover, in the second from reduced receipts, in the third from increased costs.

It is very difficult to state as a matter of theory what will be done, because no retailer can decide in advance what is most profitable for him to do. This is because the best course for any firm depends on what course his competitors are following: since this will also be true for the competitors, an element of guess-work is introduced and, in theory, we might have a state of affairs in which the prices were continually changing, each retailer altering his tactics to correspond with what his competitors were doing and then having to change it because they had changed *their* prices or selling methods as a result of *his* alterations. In practice, they would of course all learn after a time how each was likely to behave in varying circumstances, and would thus reach some empirical position of live and let live. But all such positions are empirical, in the sense that we cannot tell in advance which of the possible situations will actually be established—we need to know something else, namely, the convention of behaviour which appeals to all the competitors who remain after what may be called the period of manœuvre is over.

Further analysis requires a fuller examination of particular cases

The facts themselves become too complicated, at this point, to be capable of being reduced to any tidy set of rules. The reader must be on his guard against thinking that any analytical treatment can be exhaustive or can explain all the facts. The primary reasons for this are that each customer has his own peculiarities and that no retailer can tell what is the best course for him to pursue against competitors until he knows what they will do in response to his own actions. For a complete analysis, we should have to know the complete behaviour pattern both of buyers and of sellers. We shall therefore turn, in the next chapter, to a consideration of the main types of retail unit as a first approximation to defining the main variations in the pattern of sellers' behaviour.

APPENDIX TO CHAPTER III

NOTE ON "OVER-FULL EMPLOYMENT"

ON page 8 we referred to the Coalition Government's White Paper on Employment Policy, the basis of the present government's policy, in which the undertaking was given to maintain, in future, a high and stable[1] level of employment in this country.

There has been no need, so far, since the war, to implement this policy since inflation has prevailed (April, 1949). Inflationary conditions, which prevail when the total of spendable income exceeds the value of available consumables at current prices in which "seven billion worth of money is running after six billion worth of goods" gives rise to what may be termed "over-full" employment. With rising prices, which characterize conditions of over-full employment, producers and traders in almost any field can make profits *if they can get labour and materials.* Over-full employment is thus characterized also by bottlenecks of labour and materials.

In the course of this chapter we have considered the field of retail trading when neither boom nor slump conditions prevailed. A normal state of trade was assumed.

In this unstable world, it seems, however, important to add a note showing what modifications of the foregoing analysis are appropriate when conditions like those which have prevailed since late 1939, namely, controlled inflation, prevail. By controlled inflation is meant the presence of an excess of consumable income over the value of consumption goods at present prices (that is, an "inflationary gap") with prices over a wide field restrained by government price administration.

We will put forward the analysis in two stages. First, the position we should expect to arise if there were controlled prices but no limitation on entry into retail trade, that is, no license restriction and no rationing. Figure III. represents the manner in which selling costs would behave if the ordinary competitive

[1]Cmd. 6527 (1944), *Employment Policy,* 3.

processes were operating. Marginal selling costs represent the characteristic rising selling costs incurred to widen the fringe of customers. It will be noticed that we are dealing with the unit or independent store, for whom selling costs rise steeply. The analysis can be applied equally well to the large-scale shop if the marginal cost curve is made to fall more rapidly and to rise considerably less steeply.

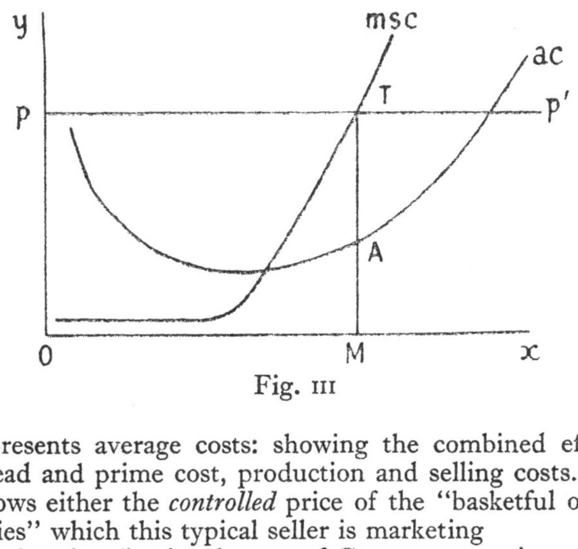

Fig. III

ac represents average costs: showing the combined effect of overhead and prime cost, production and selling costs.
pp shows either the *controlled* price of the "basketful of commodities" which this typical seller is marketing
or the situation (in the absence of Government price administration) when the seller has already taken a decision on the prices at which he will market to his existing body of custom and is solely concerned with his selling cost problem, viz., how far to increase selling costs in order to attract additional customers.

In these circumstances the quantity of commodities OM would be marketed, namely, that for which marginal selling cost=price (MT). This is the equilibrium of the firm.

Free entry would result in an influx of new traders to take advantage of the abnormal profits TA x OM. Their influx would result in a raising of costs and a lowering of prices for all competing traders until the abnormal rate of profit (TA) was obliterated. This is the equilibrium of the industry.

In over-full employment or controlled inflation, two further factors must be taken into consideration:

1. Some institutional factor may limit the amount that will be sold which was formerly determined by the equation of marginal cost and price. This factor may be either consumer rationing or merely lack of availability of supplies (the allocation of which may or may not be affected by unofficial Trade Association action or by some official "Fair Shares" scheme).

2. There may be limitation of entry; either a government scheme of licensing the opening of shops and/or the sale of particular products or, where wartime licensing (as in the non-food field in Britain) has been removed, the abnormal hindrance to entry which results from the bottleneck in premises and labour.

When these further factors are taken into consideration, the retailer's position can be illustrated as follows:

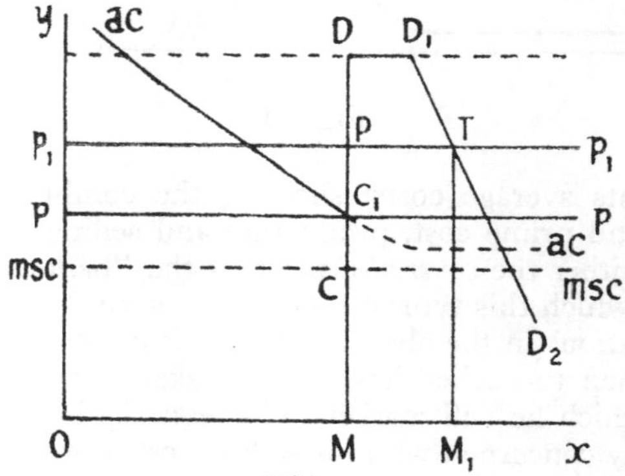

Fig. IV

p represents the old price-line (v. Figure III).

p_1 represents the new administered price. This is higher than p because where, as in this country, prices are administered by particular Maximum Price Regulations (as contrasted, for example, with the "general freeze" of prices employed during the war in the U.S.), government price administrators both in the Board of Trade and in the Ministry of Food have tended conspicuously to fix the overriding *uniform* maximum price for all traders at a level which covers the average costs of the marginal or least efficient trader.[1] Thus, we can fairly draw p_1 higher than p. The price before the emergence of "over-full" employment is p and afterwards it is p_1.

D_1D_2 slopes downward to the right and is not parallel with OX(as are p and p_1) because once the seller begins to raise prices, questions of market imperfection can no longer be assumed away. The range of the demand curve DD_1, showing perfect elasticity, denotes the delayed impact of market imperfections in inflation. DD_1D_2 intersects p_1 (the controlled price line) at T showing that the trader could sell more than OM at the controlled price; he could sell OM_1 at price p_1 (M_1T) if only he could get it. Correspondingly he could market the amount he can get (OM) at a price considerably higher (MD) than the controlled price MP: hence black market operations.

The equilibrium of the firm, in these conditions, is determined by (*a*) shortages of supplies and (*b*) limitation of entry.

The individual firm, shown in Fig. IV, supplies OM and, for that quantity, marginal cost (MC) is below price (MP) and so is average cost (MC_1).

If entry had been free, competition would now occur for registrations, where there is consumer registration, and for custom where there is none, thereby re-introducing imperfections in the market. (To the extent that traders compete for registrations *within* the limited total supply, imperfections are present.) We could draw a rising curve of marginal selling costs to represent the way in which selling costs would behave so soon as competition of this character occurred. (Where there is free entry, the analysis of Chapter III applies in full.) Some profits are then eliminated because, first, average costs would begin to rise and second, prices would fall as a result of the necessity of lowering prices to deal with "fringe" (marginal customer) difficulties.

[1]While this may well have been a suitable policy in wartime when resources, particularly labour, were taken from the distributive trades by direct mobilization, it can hardly be considered so suitable in peacetime when it tends to promote an over-expansion.

MSC, marginal selling costs, are shown constant for all ranges of output. Here is a fundamental difference between Figs. III and IV; in inflation, traders find that they can sell, at the controlled prices, all the goods on which they can lay their hands. Customers queue to obtain them. In fact, some of the "market imperfections" are eliminated. Price, as a result of price control, is prevented from performing its normal function of equating demand with supply. Prices are controlled to prevent them from reaching as high a level as they would otherwise have done. This is necessarily accompanied, in the absence of consumer rationing, by an excess demand of would-be buyers over available supplies. The condition of rising selling costs for greater sales does not, therefore, any longer prevail.

AC, average costs, fall throughout their length but never cut the marginal cost curve because marginal costs never rise. It should be emphasized at this point, that the shape of the curves beyond the point M is entirely conjectural. OM is the limit of sales because the trader cannot get anything more than OM to sell. DD_1D_2 is a segment of the ordinary demand curve showing the maximum price per unit sellers can obtain for amounts sold measured along OX.

The continuation of licensing in the field of food retailing, however, requires the application of the supplementary analysis included in this Appendix in full; and the persistence of bottlenecks in premises and labour supply (typical of inflationary conditions) requires its application over a wider field, in fact, wherever these conditions persist. In these circumstances, traders in general are in receipt of excess profits attributable directly to conditions of "over-full" employment (and the accompanying inflation) in the economy as a whole combined with the imperfections of their own markets.

CHAPTER IV

RETAIL DISTRIBUTION

Retailer maximizes profits

THE results of the analysis made in Chapter III can be summarized as follows: the trader has fundamentally two types of problem in deciding what is his best trading policy: first, to get the most profit from servicing his existing customers at any time (by equating marginal cost with marginal revenue) and secondly to increase expenditure on expanding his circle of customers (increasing goodwill) up to the profitable limit until he finds himself confronting potential buyers who are so far distant from him (either because they live so far away or are resistant to his particular selling appeals) that it would require more expenditure on salesmanship than the net receipts (total receipts minus prime costs) from their purchases.

Abnormal profits induce competition from new entrants

Wherever there is no artificial restraint on entry into the trade, the receipt of abnormally high profits in any area will induce new-comers to open shops. Once competition has appeared, the seller can no longer contemplate his fundamental problem, just described, in Chapter III, but must bear in mind the *loss* of customers which now confronts him.

How competition works

His methods of retaliation are as follows:

(1) To acquiesce: if he does not alter his selling policy, then his profits will be diminished as a result of his now reduced volume of sales (turnover).

(2) To compete by price reductions: If he reduces his prices, then his profits are reduced as the result of an immediate fall in receipts.

(3) To increase selling costs: In this case, his profits are reduced by the pressure of increased costs.

There is a fourth method by which the trader can endeavour

to avoid the contraction of his profits as a result of competition, which we did not mention in the previous chapter, though it is widely used, and that is to endeavour by political[1] action to regulate competition by such means as the following:

(*a*) The integration of trading units; in the case of horizontal integration, firms at the same trading level, whether retail, wholesale or production, combine to behave as a single trading unit. Where the combination is vertical, the combination affects traders at more than one level and sometimes also the manufacturers.

(*b*) The policy of Trade Association which is discussed in Chapter VIII.

(*c*) Legislation: In the United States, for example, political activity by certain trading groups has secured the legal prohibition of competition which was undermining their existing profit position.

At this point, it becomes necessary to abandon the simplifying assumptions of the previous chapter and to take account of the widely varying patterns of consumer and producer behaviour.

The present chapter applies the previous analysis (with necessary modifications) to the main types of trading unit at the retail level. At a later stage (Chapter V) the analysis is applied to wholesale trade. It seems preferable to begin with retailing because the organizational structure of the retail trade is more complex and also because it is, from the point of view of the resources tied up in its operations, by far the most important. There are perhaps four times as many people employed in retail as are employed in wholesale trade.

Character of retail trade

The field of retail distribution needs no introduction to the reader. All of us are almost daily the more or less willing partners in its operations: shopping is a universal necessity. Yet we should do well not to allow familiarity to breed contempt. It would be difficult to overestimate the importance of shopkeep-

[1]The term "political" is used here in its widest sense to mean the persuasion of other, hitherto independent, trading units to give up certain competitive practices and to take action against those who retain them.

ing to the real income, the standard of living, of the community. The retail distributor, the shopkeeper, being in direct contact with the consumer, has both the first and the last word in the economic causal sequence, transmitting as he does the consumers' desires, as evidenced by his daily shopping, via the wholesale distributors or direct, to the production level.

To gain profitable business, the retailer tries to sell the consumer what he wants; with the same aim in view, the wholesaler or manufacturer tries to sell the retailer what he wants and the producer, of course, tries to manufacture what he can market. The shopkeeper could thus be likened to the antennae of the economic system comprising production and distribution, were it not that in the very act of selling, the retailer influences purchasers so that he is no merely passive recipient of external stimuli and the so-called controlling power of demand is proportionately limited and the importance of marketing, that is the act of selling, is proportionately increased. The controlling power of demand, traditional in competitive theory, was held to reside in the stimulus provided by increased prices where "demand exceeded supply" and vice versa. The index of price variations in response to variations in consumer demand no longer operates where price competition has been replaced by forms of non-price competition. By the same token, advertising and branding have altered the character of salesmanship—some say they have "deskilled" the retailer, meaning that they have made his operations, where the sale of branded goods is concerned, purely repetitive.

How sensitive the shopkeepers are to the consumers' preferences is a matter for discussion. The point emphasized here is that the consumer has, by and large, no other means of registering his preferences and of getting what he wants out of the complicated production machine—millions of workers with millions of capital embodied in hands and machines, making tens of thousands of different products—than via the retailers. The efficiency of the distributors in selling any commodity is reflected back in production. In an economic system where it is still to a large extent true that production is undertaken for profit, and where resources, land, labour and capital will offer their services to the highest bidder, efficient retailing is essential if the quantities and types of consumables issuing from the productive system are to correspond at all closely to what the consumers want.

Retailing, though the word itself means to re-cut, has come to mean the conduct of a place of business where goods are sold to the ultimate consumer. Now, there are means by which the ultimate consumer can buy commodities without shopping for them. By mail-order, on the basis of a catalogue, he may order by post and receive his purchases in the same way.

Is an industrial revolution possible in the field of distribution?

House to house salesmen may call on the consumer in contrast to the usual method of the customer canvassing the shops. Or, again, automatic slot machines may by inanimate means distribute consumables to the ultimate consumer. While global figures are not available for this country, it is clear that, quantitatively speaking, by far the major part of commodities reach the ultimate consumer via the retail shops and that other methods of distribution to the ultimate consumer are, anyhow at the present time, quantitatively negligible. This is a field in which prediction is out of place. Mechanization has, as yet, scarcely affected the technique of shopkeeping. It is possible that surprising results may yet follow the introduction of machinery into the field of distribution. However, the degree to which mechanization could economically be carried in the field of distribution would always be limited by the factor mentioned in the introduction, namely, that centralized production has as its corollary decentralized distribution—someone has to get the goods to the individual doorstep. If prediction is permitted at all, then we may say that there will always be a place for the small retail distributive unit but this does not necessarily mean the non-mechanized distributive unit, as the slot machine demonstrates.

Types of retail trading unit

In examining the structure of the retail distributive trade, one gets the sensation of not being able to see the wood for the trees. Day to day familiarity with the shops makes it less likely that any but the student will stand away, as it were, to see the organization of the whole trade in perspective. At first glance, the trade may look fairly homogeneous. The casual visitor to Oxford Street is not constrained to classify the shops he sees into various types. He will not be impressed immediately with the fact that Dolcis is a chain-store and Selfridges a department store. He observes that some shops are considerably larger than others and that whereas Selfridges has some thirty windows and an impressive façade, Bumpus has only three windows and most shops have only one. At first sight, they look much the same. (The more experienced shopper will very often make straight for some particular shop because he knows its general type and he considers that type of shop suits him best. But on further acquaintance, the shopper becomes well aware of several distinct types of trading unit.) A brief identification of these types will provide us with a small glossary of terms required for a discussion of the organizational aspect of retail trading. Armed with this glossary, we can then proceed to a review of the trends in this country and in the United States during the latest period which can in any sense be called normal, that is, the inter-war period. In the course of this review some aspects of the all-important question whether retailing is efficient will come to light. Lack of statistical data for this country makes the answer largely conjectural, but wartime experience, treated in a subsequent chapter, under the pressure of necessity has provided certain empirical data; experiments were made during the war which lead relentlessly to certain conclusions. But this is anticipation. First, we must construct the glossary and examine the elementary facts.

Five types of shops, strikingly dissimilar in trading methods, can be distinguished, and, while retail shops commonly restrict their wares to a fairly definite category, or categories of commodities, there is no restriction of a given type of trading unit to a given category of commodity: all types can be found marketing all categories of commodities though there is a positive correlation between types of trading unit and commodity group in certain fields. Moreover, within these types there is a wide range of sizes, measured by turnover or any other index. Thousands of shoppers daily go straight to Marks & Spencer over and above those who happen to be passing Marks

& Spencer at the time when they formulate the desire to buy one of the objects available there. They do this because, by now, Marks & Spencer denotes a certain type of shop well known to shoppers.

Let us proceed then to continue the analysis begun in Chapter III and identify the main types of retail store. They will be found to correspond to different types of market imperfection.

We can distinguish five main types of retail trading unit:

(1) The "Independent" or "Unit" shop.
(2) The "Multiple" and "Chain" store.
(3) The "Combination" store or "Supermarket."
(4) The "Department" store.
and (5) The "Co-operative" Store.

In Chapter III, the retailer was envisaged as having a circle of custom extending from those persons who were nearest to him either geographically or in the sense of being most responsive to his particular sales techniques to those who were so far out of the retailer's reach, in either of these senses, for it to be only just worth his while to attract their custom.

I. The Independent or Unit shop

The simplest type of retailing unit is found where the cost of selling rises steeply as the circle which the retailer wishes to attract gets larger. This will happen if customers like personal shopping but do not like the trouble of going some distance: or if delivery costs rise steeply: or if customers have very sharply distinguished personal tastes, so that the outlay necessary to overcome existing consumer attachments, whether by advertising or by the provision of some other form of service, is large.

It has often been said and remains true that retailing is, from the point of view of the total number of shops, the province of the small man. This applies both to the United Kingdom and to the United States. The so-called Unit shop, the traditional type of shop carried on as an independent business drawing custom primarily from the immediate neighbourhood represented "perhaps ninety per cent of all shops"[1] in Britain

[1]Retail Trade Committee, *2nd Interim Report* (1942), 4.

on the outbreak of war. The United States Census of Business shows that 1,521,145 out of 1,770,355 (86 per cent.) were of this type in 1939[1] exactly the same percentage for that country in 1939. This type of store, however, only marketed perhaps 50 per cent of the total retail turnover in Britain (1939) and some 65.2 per cent of total retail sales (1939) in the United States. Two main sub-types may be distinguished:

Different types of independent or unit shop

(*a*) The shop in the main street, often of considerable size, employing a staff of one or more assistants and perhaps providing credit and delivery services.

(*b*) The shop in the side street, run as a whole-time or part-time occupation without assistance from outside though with help from members of the family and drawing custom entirely from the immediate neighbourhood. Credit may be given but delivery service is unimportant.[2]

Into one or other of these categories of "independent" shop fall the vast majority of retailers. The independent "unit" shop has virtues from the customer's and thus from the economic point of view which other forms of retail trading unit do not afford in equal measure. Such is proximity. Tens of thousands of these small shops are scattered all over the country. They sell to the neighbourhood. Now the customer can either travel to the central shops of a town or city or buy from the shop around the corner. In either case, and this is a point of importance, the cost of travel is there. It may be that the customer pays for it in the price he pays the retailer, and he thus indirectly pays the neighbourhood shopkeeper for getting the food for him, or he himself spends time, energy and his bus fare in getting to the central store. Many prefer the former alternative. Furthermore, the neighbourhood shopkeeper has usually some personal interest in his customers which the customer is unlikely to sense in the large chain or department store where he is one among thousands of daily customers.

[1]*Sixteenth Census of the United States* (1940) *Census of Business*, Vol. I, 48 and 63, Table 3a. The category "independents" includes also multi-unit, market and roadside stands and leased dependents. Single-store independents numbered 1,521,145 out of a total of 1,770,355 retail stores of all kinds.

[2]Retail Trade Committee, *2nd Interim Report*, 4.

We said above that selling costs would rise steeply where:

(1) customers liked personal shopping but did not like the trouble of going some distance and/or

(2) delivery costs rose steeply and/or

(3) customers had sharply distinguished personal tastes so that the outlay necessary to overcome existing consumer attachments was large. (The fact that the small shop meets these consumer preferences better than any other constitutes an irrefutable economic case for the small independent store: but not, be it emphasized, for the numbers of these stores presently in existence, nor for the precise trading methods which they currently employ. We shall return to these points at a later stage.)

Thus we get the cost of selling rising steeply as the "independent" shopkeeper trespasses the bounds of those who live nearby or are tied to him by personal acquaintance. The shopkeeper spends a good deal of time suiting each customer's personal idiosyncrasies. People who enjoy that kind of attention buy from this kind of store by preference. The shops are small-scale so the economy of overheads is insufficient to compensate for rising marginal selling costs. Delivery services, where they are provided, would show steeply rising costs after the one delivery boy or the one delivery vehicle was fully occupied. Great prospective gain would be required to induce the retailer to employ an additional delivery boy or delivery vehicle and this great gain is not, in the circumstances of the case, forthcoming.

Little capital is necessary to set up such a shop. The retailer can normally obtain his stock-in-trade on credit from the wholesaler (see Chapter V). If he belongs to the second type[1] he can, if necessary, at little expense convert part of his own dwelling into a shop. Or, if to the first type,[1] his rent will be considerably lower than if his premises were located in a fashionable shopping centre. He can himself, by himself, run the shop or the wife can mind the shop while the husband does other work or draws unemployment insurance.

There is, normally[2] no limitation on entry and, as we said

[1]See page 55.
[2]Subject now, in Britain, to the requirements of town planning.

above, little initial capital is required. If, in any area, shopkeepers of this type are making high profits, new-comers will enter, as it were in between existing shops until eventually each retailer will have only enough business to cover his costs and allow him to keep going. It should be noticed that this position is consistent with differences in gross profits and retail margins *and in retail prices*, as it is not likely that customers will be evenly spread either in space or in their range of taste, but no firm would be able to get more than twice[1] as much net profits as anyone else, as this would induce a competitor into his particular area or type of service. The extra profits arise from what economists call "indivisibility": the market is bunchy and the size of the firm necessary to earn any profits at all is too large for there to be a spread of these firms closely corresponding to the spread of consumers.

Such a situation might arise when there were a number of small towns evenly dispersed. In this case, we should expect to find perhaps only one shop of a particular kind in each town: each shop would be protected from its competitors by the trouble of going to another town. But since this would always be possible, there are limits to the prices that can be charged by any shop. If profits become too high, either because the size of the town increases or because the protection of distance allows an individual shop to charge exorbitant prices, even before the degree of excess profit became sufficient to induce the establishment of an additional shop, some other *type* of trading might take some of the trade—for example a mail order firm—thus setting up, as it were, between existing firms.

It should be noted that the existence of normal profits for all traders is, in view of the inherent "bunchiness" of the market, not inconsistent with the charging of varying retail prices and margins, nor with the receipt of different rates of profit by traders.

The small-scale shopkeeper's business methods

Returning to the four possible methods of reaction to competition; what is the typical reaction in practice of this type of trading unit?

[1]cf. 35 above.

(1) The small shops, to a large extent, acquiesce in the loss of customers. With reduced turnover they hang on, often with a miserable standard of living. In the case of the small shop in the side street, the master tends to reduce the supply price of his own labour to a level of income that no Wages Council would condone! His is the freedom to accept, being self-employed, a sub-standard of living. Very often, the owners do not know precisely how low it is because they keep no accounts.

Cadbury[1] (Industrial Record) refers to a substantial number of shops with a total turnover of £20-£40 a week. Shops with a turnover of less than £15 a week or even £10 a week were "distressingly numerous." From this sum must be subtracted the cost of the goods and all the retailer's other expenses before an idea can be got of the sum left over for the living expenses of himself and his family—Cadbury adds that in such cases, the shop was seldom the proprietor's sole means of support.

Can this situation be desirable from the consumer's point of view either? Can it really be argued that the consumer really prefers having a number of, let us say, petrol stations close to one another, none fully used, rather than a small number fully used which could afford to reduce their charges in view of their larger turnover?

Cadbury's view is: It was impossible to escape the broad conclusion that there were everywhere too many shops, little difference being shown in this respect between town and country or between large and small towns.[2]

There is ample evidence, to be seen on all sides, that our analysis is realistic. We might perhaps once more quote the judgment of Cadbury Brothers,[3] after careful investigation of the confectionery selling points in six widely various areas, that "In general, competition between shops was such, in the inter-war period, that the average reward of the shopkeeper was by no means high, and failure was very common among those who had miscalculated their chances or who had set up business without any knowledge, or who had less than the ordinary skill and aptitude for shopkeeping. On the other hand, the prizes

[1]Cadbury Brothers, Ltd., *Industrial Record*, 1919-39.
[2]Cadbury Brothers, Ltd., id.
[3]Cadbury Brothers, Ltd., id.

obtainable by those who were able to formulate and give effect to new ideas, were substantial." Into this last category fall the organizational types to which we proceed later in this chapter.

(2) In the case where price cuts are used to meet competition, the effect is to decrease the outlay each retailer can *afford* to reach the customers least attracted to him by situation or taste so that his circle of customers will shrink as his prices fall. Meanwhile, his nearest competitors will find that their costs rise as they try to reach farther into his territory so that they have to call a halt at some point.

(3) The third case was that in which the retailer met competition by increasing his selling costs. It seems at first sight that since he was previously spending on selling his goods all that it paid him to do, he will make no change in this respect. If, however, the new firms have overlapped on his territory, it will probably seem to them that they can detach some of his customers by special selling efforts, and he will be forced to meet this or to lose his trade. The position will then be somewhat unstable, each of the competitors now trying to enlarge his sales by special services, now finding that this is costing more than it is worth. Sooner or later, however, each will be forced to adopt a policy which is consistent with that being pursued by the others (for otherwise the situation would never settle, and in practice it always does so): and this must be one in which the overlapping customers are shared more or less by chance among all the firms who have access to them. Each firm will have its own special circle of those who are firmly attached to it, and a share of the remainder, who may be either attached though lightly, or distributing their custom indifferently.

(4) It is not necessary, however, for competition to take the form of price cuts or increased selling costs. In many cases, manufacturers' trade associations with and without the agreement of retail and wholesale traders, have adopted the device of fixing the retail price of their goods and refusing to supply goods at all to any shop which cuts this price. In other cases, the retailers themselves have agreed either as a result of past experience of the dangers of price wars, or because of a sense

that they ought to get something from each customer towards their overheads, on a particular price, or more commonly a particular mark-up. This has the same effect as price maintenance imposed by manufacturers. In both cases, the retailer is compelled, from external constraint or from a feeling of expediency or propriety to refrain from price competition.

In all cases, each firm must be getting less trade than before the competitive process began, and once more getting either normal profits, or something more because of a bunchiness in its custom, yet not large enough to make it worth while for another retailer to break into the circle. The profits are smaller, not only because there is less turnover for each firm, but also because of any additional selling expenses to which all firms have been put during the period of active competition, and which they have not yet abandoned. It is true that if they all abandoned these expenses at the same time, they would all be better off, though they would still have the danger of more firms coming in. But no one firm is likely to make a start, since if it did so, another which did not follow it would get extra customers. It is, therefore, unlikely that any firm *will* start, and oligopoly, when individual traders take into account the reaction of others to changes in their selling policy, is thus seen to be inherent in the retail market.

The situation described in the preceding paragraph is a very common one, and is especially characteristic of those parts of retail trade where price maintenance is imposed by manufacturers. New firms come in, and all firms have to spend various amounts on services, advertising, etc., until the trade settles down to a quiet life with no outstanding profits; the combined effect of smaller turnover and higher costs has eliminated them, except so far as they are due to "indivisibilities."[1] From the customers' point of view, this situation is worse than the previous one, where competition took the form of price cuts. For,

[1]The smaller the size of firm, the less will be their differences in profits. The term "indivisibilities" refers, in economics, to the fact that economic quantities such as firms and units of output, are not in practice, infinitely divisible. Thus, to induce new entrants, profits must be to a greater or less extent above the normal level according to the economic scale of operations of the would-be entrants.

in this case, the customer has not been given the option: he might prefer to pay more and get a larger number of shops and more "service" in one form or another, but so long as price maintenance is enforced there is no way of finding out if this is really so, since he is deprived of the alternative of getting the articles more cheaply.

Points to be noticed are that, contrary to the competitive assumption, uniform retail prices are a symptom of various forms of collusion among sellers; furthermore, that monopolistic competition with oligopoly, as seen in this field, provides irresistible incentive to the proscription of price competition by some form of agreement among sellers whereupon competition in terms of a variety of so-called "services" takes its place; lastly, that where net profits are above "normal" there will be an immediate intrusion of new-comers so that if by any means like resale price maintenance or inflation net profits are increased, this will lead directly to a multiplication of "independent" retail outlets. We shall refer to these interim conclusions in making our final estimate.

The numerical preponderance of this type of organizational unit was not reflected in an equivalent proportion of the total retail business. Furthermore it is clear, though the Retail Trade Committee makes no estimate, that by far the largest part of this trade was undertaken by the first of our sub-categories above, the larger independent in the main street and that the volume of trade done by each family shop is small. Reasons will be put forward, however, at a later stage for supposing that the importance of this type of unit in its effect on the level of price-maintained prices is more important than the volume of business would suggest.

In both countries both their absolute and relative numbers were well maintained. In Britain it is held that the percentage of total retail business conducted by this type of unit declined somewhat in the inter-war period. In the United States, it declined from 68.7 per cent. in 1929 to 64.9 per cent in 1935 but *rose* again in 1939 to 65.2 per cent. From the point of view of numbers, this type of store has maintained its position; out of a total number of stores 1,770,355 in 1939, they comprised 1,521,145 (85 per cent); out of a total of 1,587,718 in 1935, they comprised 1,354,196 (85 per cent) and in 1929, out of a total of 1,543,158 they comprised 1,310,695 (85 per cent).[1]

Large-scale retail business

We will leave the "unit" or independent firm at this point and proceed to the far different patterns of business behaviour which appear when trading is done on a large scale. A different case arises where the economies to be got from doing business on a large scale are great enough to outweight the costs of obtaining additional customers. It will now pay the retailer to expand until he occupies the whole market in which this condition applies, that is until the cost of selling to new customers is again more than the price they will pay, the condition already analysed. During the process of expansion, however, the expanding retailer will be able to undersell any competitors he encounters since every customer he manages to detach will lower his costs and increase those of the retailer from whom the customer was detached. Thus a monopoly would be established, and at first sight we would expect that this would go on as long as the price charged was low enough to keep out the firms which had been wiped out during the expansion. But if the profits are big enough, there will be as always inducement to enter the field: this time, however, entry will take place, *not* as before at sites or using selling methods as far removed as possible from those of existing firms, but in as close proximity as possible to the existing undertaking. For it wants to enter the same market, and the wider its range the lower its costs: the new firms try to establish themselves by price competition, or even by close imitation of the methods of the first firm, hoping that chance will provide their share of the market. The main problem will be to get going at all, since in the circumstances stated there are bound to be losses in the early stages when turnover is low and costs, therefore, high: for this reason, a large initial capital will be needed to set up a business of this kind.

Rapid change will take place in the structure of trade when there is a sudden change in transport or other selling costs or when one competitor discovers some method of business which

[1]*Sixteenth Census of the United States* (1940) *Census of Business.*

has a new kind of appeal and which, therefore, enables him to get a great many new customers at small cost to himself. In the retail trade a good example is the great growth, especially in the United States and in the Dominions, of the mail order house, which was suddenly able to offer a great variety of goods usually at marked price reductions, to a wide range of customers who had previously been served by a large number of country stores. The only advantages retained by the country store were that the customer could see the goods, that if he liked the storekeeper he could have a conversation with him and perhaps with other shoppers, and that if he could not wait even for the few days necessary for the post, he could get something at once. These advantages did not prevent the mail order house from taking away a great deal of the trade that was once done locally. It is also clear that there is in most countries enough business to support several mail order houses, generally situated in the largest towns and adopting almost identical methods. With the growth of towns, however, and also with the increase in consumers' incomes, customers are able both to see a larger stock in local shops and to be able to afford to indulge their individual tastes, and mail order houses gradually lose their pre-eminence, as they have to a remarkable extent in England and to a lesser extent in the United States. They have never been so important in England, where towns are large and transport easy, as they have overseas. Probably the best example of the situation we have in mind was the growth of the chain and multiple stores.

II. Multiple and Chain Stores

The chain store represents centralized buying combined with decentralized selling; one firm owns and operates on very similar lines a number of retail shops combining the economies of large-scale ordering and standardized methods, with a wide distribution of retail outlets so that it is something like a mail order house, with the advantage that the goods can be seen and bought at once. In the early days of chain stores, very great economies were made through bulk buying of an aggressive and imaginative kind, which enabled the stores to break right through consumer resistance by price cuts so large that the goods sold themselves and indeed created such an atmosphere of cheapness that many lines could be sold on a large scale even though the price cuts were small or non-existent. There was thus a period of transition, during which the proportion of retail business conducted by the chain store increased rapidly.

As in the case of the independent shop there are here two main sub-categories: the "variety" chain deals in a wide range of goods limited only by the self-imposed proviso that they can be produced at a price enabling them to be retailed at a certain figure: the multiple store, a chain of shops specializing in a restricted range of goods.

What does this mean from the point of view of the shopper? It means first that he knows nothing in Marks & Spencer will cost him more than, say, ten shillings and nothing in Woolworth will cost him more than two shillings and sixpence. Pre-war, every branch of Woolworth had printed in large letters over the shop front, the price limit of sixpence and in America, customers still speak of the "Five and Ten." During the war, as prices rose and the universal scarcity of consumables increased, the price limits for a single article[1] were raised and the caption was painted out, but the policy remained identical in principle although the actual price ranges had been increased, and the body of shoppers knew it.

Such a price policy has great attractions for the shopper. He avoids the embarrassment of being confronted with merchandise which he cannot afford to buy. He knows where he is.

How does "centralized buying and decentralized selling" affect the shopping public? Centralized buying results firstly in the centralized control of shop design and operation. All the branches of Marks & Spencer or Woolworth, look the same, have the same type of shop front and the same internal disposal, the same type of equipment and correspondingly, the same general methods of sale. This again has a great appeal to the shopper. One of the outstanding characteristics of the modern shopper is that providing he has the sensations of freedom of choice, he is happy to be deprived of the burdensome task of

[1]The words "single article" are meant not to exclude the system, widely used, of selling articles composed of several parts, like a standard lamp so long as the price of each constituent part (standard, bulb, shade and cord) did not exceed the voluntarily imposed limit.

weighing a variety of imponderable evidence. He likes, to an unknown but important extent, to surrender freedom of choice. One of the arts of salesmanship is to know how far and in what respects he likes to do this. It is not to no purpose that a continually increasing number of young economists, fresh from Universities and Colleges are being employed in so-called market-research; so little of any precision, so far, is known about such consumer propensities as these, yet the discovery of even one such may prove to be exceedingly profitable to the maker and simultaneously, it should be observed, to the consuming public.

Centralized buying includes not only the buying of equipment and thus indirectly the shaping of sales policy for all branches, but the purchase of the goods to be retailed, of the stock in trade. The Chain Stores buy directly from the manufacturers, thereby eliminating the wholesaler. The substance of Chapter V combined with the discussion earlier in the present chapter of the functions of the small independent retailer, will be sufficient to show that the reader should not deduce from the substantial price reductions which the Chain Stores are able to offer on account of the economies of centralized purchase and of large-scale operations in general, that the wholesaler's operations are redundant. If it were true that shops of the chain store type could "economically" take over the whole of retail business being undertaken at the present time by the "unit" shops such a deduction might be made. But it is part of the imperfection of this market that the unit shop should have alternative virtues which are preferred by some consumers and so are justified from the economic point of view.

We have dealt so far with the so-called Variety Chain Store which, as its name implies, does not concentrate on a single category of goods, but normally sells at the same time, food, hardware, stationery, clothing and a wide range of miscellaneous goods. There is no need to elaborate their selling operations in more detail since most readers are familiar with this type of shop. If not, Marks & Spencer or Woolworth have branches all over the country for their investigation.

Their main appeal is a price appeal and this type of shop provides little in the way of elaborate consumer services like wrappings, or credit, elegant shoppers' rest rooms or commissionaires.

Multiple Store

Very similar from the point of view of trade policy, but differing in its concentration on a narrower range of commodities is the Multiple shop. Multiple shops are based on the idea of setting up a chain of shops and specializing in a relatively limited range of goods.

Multiple shops such as Lipton and Sainsbury are well known in the food field, where this type of unit plays an important part. It is by no means restricted to the field of food, however, and there are well-known multiples in the footwear, drug, men's outfitting, furniture and hardware sections. The Retail Trade Committee reports that "Multiple shops exist in practically all trades."

The Multiple shops have a similar appeal to the consumer as the Variety Chain Stores and the only substantial differences are those which result from concentration on a narrower range of goods, that is, the shopper will not go to a Multiple shop to find all he wants under one roof.

That the chain and multiple stores achieve substantial economies in cost from buying direct from the manufacturer cannot be doubted. The main appeal of this type of store is a price appeal, good value for money. Bulk purchase gives the retailer sufficient bargaining power with the manufacturer to secure the observance of such quality standards as he cares to impose.

In the United States the emergence of this new type of trading unit in the last decade of the nineteenth century was followed by a period of dramatic growth. The period of most rapid expansion in that country appears to have been between 1906—1929,[1] and the number of stores grew even faster than the number of firms showing a tendency to concentration of management. The chains reached the climax of their development, in the sense of effecting maximum proportion of aggregate retail sales for the country as a whole, around 1933. Previously to that time, in the terms of our analysis, the rapid

[1]Bellamy, *Institute of Statistics Bulletin* (1946), Nos. 8, 10, 11.

extension of the use of the motor-car by all classes in the U.S. had made selling costs rise much less steeply: a factor favouring larger scale enterprise. By 1933 the main adaptations consequent on this change in people's mobility had been made. Meantime the chain itself had given rise to a revolution in the selling *methods* of the independents to which we shall refer in our treatment of the so-called "super-market".

During the period 1918-28 the chains and multiples were growing rapidly in Britain and Bellamy estimates that the rate of closing of chains was only one quarter of their rate of opening —showing how rapidly their numbers were expanding. These comparative rates contrast with a rate of entry for independents which was roughly equivalent to the rate of closure; so that the total numbers remained constant. The proportion of total retail sales effected by the chain stores continued to increase between 1929 and 1935 from 20.6 per cent to 23.3 per cent. Thereafter, the proportion decreased to 21 per cent in 1939; clearly, the overlap with other types of retail trader, particularly the independent trader, was encountered about the mid 1930s and the task of increasing the *aggregate* business of the chains became an increasingly expensive problem. This did not mean that particular firms were unable progressively to increase their business.

III Combination Store or Super-market—American experience

The competition of a new type of trading unit, itself arising in no small measure from the competition of the chains, was partly responsible for the most outstanding development in America during the inter-war period, which was the growth of a new type of retail trading unit, the "combination store" or "super-market" trading typically in groceries and meats.

In 1929, this type of trading unit accounted for 36 per cent of the total food business and by 1939 for as much as 54 per cent. It is typically a large cash and carry food store with a turnover of more than $100,000 per annum. The main feature is the exercise of individual selection without sales-people: the customer goes into the shop through a grill and he is free to select his own merchandise from open shelves (except where cutting is required) entirely without the service of salespeople. Conveyances on wheels (rather like perambulators) are available to the customer on which he can place his purchases as he buys them. Finally when he has completed his purchases, he detaches the tray upon which he has placed his accumulated purchases, puts it on a counter by the next grill, whereupon the total expenditure is computed by a clerk and payment is made in cash. If services are made available an extra charge is usually made for them.

There are only a few instances of this type of unit in Britain.[1] It is a striking example of the substitution of simple, inexpensive mechanical devices for labour. Anyone using these must be impressed by the manner in which the customer is provided with the services he needs and not compelled to pay for those he does not. The main waste in retailing, the fact that salesmen have to stand altogether idle in "off hours" and at all times while the customer is contemplating the available merchandise and making up his mind, is avoided by this means.

The super-market in the United States has, in the main, either put the old-style country store, stocking mixed merchandise both food and non-food, out of business by force of competition or, equally frequently, by providing the *pattern* on which they have been reorganized. Thus we have competition from a different type of trading unit leading to a modernization amounting to a technical revolution in the selling methods of another trading type—the independent store. This technical revolution, together with the introduction of labour-saving sales techniques described above, has also been characterized by a tendency towards greater specialization: the combination store normally concentrates on either food or merchandise.

The success of these trading methods has been remarkable in the U.S. The number of combination stores has increased by ten per cent in ten years (1929-1939). As a result the survival value of the independent store, in the face of competition from chain and multiple, large-scale traders, has been enormously strengthened.

[1]Marks and Spencer operate a unit of this kind in London and the Co-operative Societies have recently started several.

IV. Department Store

Our fourth type of retail distributing unit is the Department Store. Like the chain store types, it achieves the economies of large-scale distribution, notably those of centralized purchase. But whereas the chain store extends its field of operations over a number of shopping districts (albeit with standardized merchandise sold in standardized distributive units), the department store sells a wide variety of merchandise under one roof. It establishes, in its departments, a number of single shops, as it were, under one roof. Each department normally has a "buyer" at the head who is responsible both for the buying of his department and for its selling policy. Laurence Neal[1] comments on this arrangement that it fails to make the most of the possible economies of centralized purchase and while it provides a certain discipline in so far as the man who buys the goods for his department is also responsible for selling them, it is contrary to the fullest application of the principle of the division of labour. In contradistinction to this general policy, one large department store employs one buyer who controls the buying of merchandise for all its stores; thus, in this instance, a department store has adopted one of the devices of a chain.

The department store type of unit is based on the principle that it is easier to sell more goods to the same customer by providing a wide range of merchandise both with regard to type and price-range, than to find more customers in a given locality to purchase the same kind of merchandise. The department store, says the Retail Trade Committee, "is based on the principle of drawing custom from a wide area to a central store which can meet all ordinary shopping needs. Everything is done to encourage customers to come to the store, and credit and delivery and other services are fully developed. . . ." In the inter-war period, however, the department stores have certainly both in this country and the United States felt the competition of the chain stores very keenly and they have, as Laurence Neal observes, responded by integration: they have increased their market turnover over which their overheads are spread by

[1] Neal, *Retailing and the Public* (1932).

integration: thus Harrods controls Dickins and Jones and D. H. Evans.

V. Co-operative Retail Store

Our fifth organizational type is the co-operative retail stores. The growth of the co-operative retail societies is a further dramatic illustration of the proposition that in the field of retail trade, a good idea can be very lucrative indeed. This idea, in the case of the co-operative societies, is that of the dividend on purchases, the co-operative "divi", a trade practice or selling device which was first practised, successfully, by the Rochdale pioneers in 1844.[1]

There are two aspects of the co-operative movement; one relates to the particular social ideal which it embodies; the second relates to the particular commercial and organization techniques which it employs. We shall deal more particularly with the second. During this century, the ideological as opposed to the commercial importance of co-operation has progressively diminished.[2]

The consumers' co-operatives are voluntary organizations controlled by the consumers. They aim at engaging in the production, wholesaling and retailing of consumption goods. It is at the retail level that the co-operatives have had their most spectacular success. At retail, the movement consisted in 1945 of 1,070 absolutely separate and autonomous retail distributive societies. These societies vary greatly in size. At that date, the 35 largest societies, with a membership of between 20,000-50,000 comprised 41.8 per cent of the total membership.

The total retail trade of the co-operatives for 1945 was

[1]Carr-Saunders, Florence and Peers *Consumers' Co-operation in Great Britain* (1942) record that the device of a dividend on purchases was used prior to 1844, on the inspiration of Owen and his followers, but the conditions for successful 'working class movements', as it then was, awaited the increasing prosperity of the second half of the nineteenth century.

[2]Hough, writing in *Store* (March, 1945).

This is understandable when the Labour Party has successfully espoused the wide social causes which the early co-operators had at heart. It is, nevertheless, to be regretted in a different context, namely the intractable problem of a wasteful use of resources owing to the imperfection of retail markets. Co-operative trading should provide an ideal for its members no less inspiring though more difficult to comprehend than the social ideals of a century ago, namely, distribution conducted for the benefit of the consumers.

£361 million and Hough estimates that it had probably risen to £400 million in 1946. This figure can be compared with a total consumers' expenditure estimated at £6,584 million for 1946.[1] The total trade was distributed among the societies roughly according to their membership. It is interesting to reflect on this fact in relation to the retailer's double problem of increasing sales to existing members as against attracting new customers; it looks as though his total turnover is likely to be more appreciably increased by the latter than by the former method.

The institutional aspect of co-operation is governed by the Industrial and Provident Societies Act of 1893 as amended by the Acts of 1913 and 1928.[2] The organizational structure of the retail societies is not as varied as their size. Each society has one or more retail shops. The affair of management is in the hands of a Committee of Management elected by the vote of members, in the proportion of one vote to each member, and by full-time salaried shopkeepers and assistants. Top policy decisions can only be made at the quarterly or annual General Meetings of members. Such decisions are the allocation of profits. The co-operative retail societies can accept share capital up to any total but no individual is allowed to hold more than £200 of share capital in any one society. Loan capital can be accepted from members or non-members. There is no statutory limit to the total of loan capital but each society determines such a maximum in its Rules.

From the total receipts of retail sales, after trading costs have been met, funds allocated to reserves, and the distribution of interest on share capital, the rest of the trading surplus is distributed among members in proportion to their purchases.

An excellent account of the Co-operative Movement is given in a volume entitled *Consumers' Co-operation in Great Britain* by Carr-Saunders, Florence and Peers. The two points of major interest from the point of view of the economies of distribution, are first, to determine the occasion for the remarkable growth of this particular type of trading unit and secondly,

[1]Cmd. 7099 (1947), *National Income and Expenditure in the United Kingdom.*
[2]See Carr-Saunders, Florence and Peers; id., 53.

to provide a definition, from the point of view of economic analysis, of the "divi". Is it, or is it not a profit? This is a question which has exercised the mind of economist, lawyer and tax authority for some time.

The growth of retail co-operation has been remarkable: from a membership of half a million in 1880 to over one and a half million members in 1900; from two and a half million members in 1910 to four and a half million ten years later until by 1935 it comprised 7,500,000 members with average annual purchases of £29 9s. 0d. per member.[1] When it is remembered that the family is normally the purchasing unit, this seven and a half million members represents more than the same number of mouths. Admittedly, co-operating families do not by any means buy all their purchases at the "co-op"; but out of eleven million families, in 1935, it is estimated that some six million were associated with the co-operative retail societies.[2] In 1939, the Board of Trade's Retail Trade Committee estimated that some ten per cent of the total retail trade was transacted by the co-ops., the largest proportion being food. The co-operatives themselves have announced that one quarter of the population registered with them for sugar.

To what is this striking achievement due?

On the cost side, there is no doubt that the retail societies achieve economies by buying from the Co-operative Wholesale Societies. Secondly, there is available an ample supply of inexpensive capital. Since 1876, one society can be a member of another and to such a case the £200 limit on personal shareholders does not apply. The co-operatives can rely on mutual finance of this character. In our analysis of the economies of large-scale, as contrasted with small scale business, we observed that sizeable initial capital was required to start operations. This factor presents no obstacle to the co-operative store.

The co-operative stores within one society resemble the chain stores in having several retail stores within one firm. In contrast to the chains, however, they do not tend to specialize. One co-operative society endeavours to supply many of the shoppers' requirements within its one building. Correspond-

[1]Carr-Saunders, Florence and Peers, id., 63, Figure 3.
[2]Carr-Saunders, Florence and Peers, id., 74.

ingly, co-operative stores have arranged to share out their particular market. This is an enormous competitive advantage since they can achieve all the economies of scale without fear of intrusion of other large-scale business near by, *within* their particular field of consumer preference.

Competing traders have asserted with vehemence that the exemption from taxation of the co-operative dividend has enormously strengthened the bargaining power of the co-operatives. Funds put to reserves are taxed as are those of any other firm; but whereas the dividends paid to shareholders in a joint stock company are taxed at source, the dividend on co-operators' purchase remains untaxed.

Mcgregor in his *Enterprise, Purpose and Profit* has detailed the various arguments, pro and con, which have been brought forward concerning the true economic character of the "divi". The more pertinent are as follows:

First, it is argued that the divi cannot be a profit because the societies could themselves abolish it overnight by selling at cost. It is therefore not of the nature of a profit, but rather of a "consumer's surplus" accruing as a result of a particular method of doing business.

Secondly, an argument closely related to the first, it is held that the "divi" is not a profit because it is the return of an overcharge. Thus, if five men contributed £10 each toward a tour which they were jointly making and the costs turned out to be no more than £40 whereupon they each received £2 change, could this latter sum then appropriately be regarded as a profit?

Third, in the corpus of ideas inspired by the term mutuality, which has been cited as grounds for tax-exemption, Macgregor distinguishes two main underlying ideas; one, that a man cannot trade with himself and the second relates to motive: the co-operatives are not run for profit.

In reply to this last, it must be countered that the co-operative society not being an individual can hardly be deemed to be an individual trading with himself and taxation is levied on individuals. Secondly, that motives are not in other contexts deemed appropriate criteria for defining economic categories of income.

The first and second arguments are more plausible at first sight. But on further investigation, particularly in the light of the above analysis of market imperfections, they are seen to contain a serious flaw; suppose that the co-operatives did sell at cost, who can suppose that the volume of co-operative sales would remain the same? Would not some of their particular clientele, attracted by the dividend on purchase, transfer their custom elsewhere after its removal? It seems more in accordance with the principles of market imperfection to determine, with Macgregor:

"Subject to market conditions which determine its scope, dividend is a trade practice or device, the effect of which is to create (together with the influence of the co-operative ideal) a measure of preferential buying, and so a greater volume of sales."

The payment of the co-operative dividend[1] can thus be likened to a particular form of selling technique with this major difference that, unlike most others, it costs nothing. It is a return partly for using the co-operative and thereby giving it a bigger turnover and affording it the economies of large-scale operation, partly for the willingness to accept less service and to pay cash and carry the goods away. The customer, when the divi is taken into account, pays less for many of his goods, but in a manner which itself causes consumer attachment.[2]

[1]Reference is made below to the particular advantage gained in many instances by the co-operatives where resale price maintenance is practised.

[2]Owing to limitations of space, the important part played by the co-operative stores in distribution has been no more than sketched in the present volume. The volume referred to by Carr-Saunders, Florence and Peers, gives a full and excellent treatment of this subject.

CHAPTER V

THE THEORY OF WHOLESALE DISTRIBUTION

THE aim of the present chapter is to consider where the wholesaler fits into the general pattern of distribition.

Specialization of function within the distributive trades

The distributive process itself is a continuous one, involving all the participants between the primary producer and the consumer-growers, manufacturers, importers, wholesalers and retailers.

The Distributive functions

The functions which are involved are the following:

(*a*) The holding of stocks and the supply of credit facilities.
(*b*) The assortment of commodities produced into marketable shapes and sizes.
(*c*) The spreading of information.
(*d*) The transport of commodities to be sold from the point of production to the point of consumption.

Someone must perform these functions or they will be left undone. In theory, anyone in the chain could undertake some part or all of the processes, and our problem is to decide whether any of them are particularly suitable for the wholesaler, whether there are distinctive functions which he can perform more cheaply than anyone else.

Illustration of the principles involved

In the simplest conceivable economy, where the individual family, alone on an island, let us say, ministers to its own needs, these distributive functions will largely be performed simultaneously with the production functions.

The spreading of information about the availability of consumer goods would provide little difficulty where the principal subject of family discussion would naturally tend to be what each member had been able to contribute during the day to the sustenance of the family. In these circumstances, all members of the family (the producers) will proudly produce in the evening what they have found or made during the day. The assortment of commodities into marketable sizes and shapes and the provision of credit facilities are not necessary in this Crusoe economy. But, even here, distinct distributive functions are likely to emerge in so far as the holding of stocks and the transport of commodities from the point of production to the point of consumption will, at an early stage, present a distinct set of problems. The efficiency of the family economy will be very much increased once some means are found, for instance, of avoiding the necessity for each individual to punctuate his day's work with interruptions designed to satisfy the immediate need for food. Stocks of food will be accumulated.[1] Probably some member of the household, the housewife, will be charged with particular responsibility for seeing that there is always something to eat and drink in the house. She will then find that prudence requires her to keep reserves or stocks, that is, a quantity over and above current requirements, sufficient to meet not only normal, anticipated requirements but also something over and above this amount in case of unexpectedly large demands or the late arrival of supplies. Specialization of function, that is, deputing one job to one member of the family and another to another, may be decided upon. The most efficient division of labour will be found when everyone is concentrating on the work for which he is best fitted, when those with the strongest physique do the heavier jobs and the women, perhaps, concentrate on the more distinctly service as opposed to manufacturing functions. Thus a crude division of labour emerges and the necessity for the performance of typically distributive functions, transport and stockholding emerges at a very early stage of economic development.

Consumers' tendency to delegate the activity of selection

Economic progress takes place through the extension of the division of labour, and in the modern world this has brought

[1]These stocks are needed because it is inconvenient to consume continuously. Discontinuous production, as in the case of crops, also requires stockholding.

with it the whole apparatus of the distributive trades. The final consumer can now buy goods as, when and where he wants them and is prepared to pay anything, it appears, from a third to a half and often considerably more of the final selling-price of consumables[1] for the services which provide this convenience. In addition, the consumer in Western civilizations is tending to allow the specialist to take over to some extent another function besides those listed at the beginning of the chapter, the exercise of consumers' choice itself. Traditional theory assumes that every buyer compares the various possible purchases carefully in order to get the best possible combination of goods, but this is often too much of a task for him.

The customer, more often than not, asks the advice of the salesman as to what he shall buy. The salesman is successful in proportion as he persuades the customer that he has bought what he wanted.

This tendency for the consumer to delegate the exercise of consumer's choice has produced divergent developments. In some fields it has brought about the increasing expertness of shop assistants; traders have been willing to employ skilled and therefore well-paid personnel to exercise the arts of persuasion. In the field of standardized, highly advertised, branded articles, it has brought about, in contrast, what amounts to a de-skilling of the shop assistant. Anyone can hand over the counter a packet of Kellogg's corn flakes and charge the listed price for it.

It should be added that the progressive tendency towards product differentiation and the abandonment of price-competition evidenced in the widespread availability of "branded" goods, has made it almost impossible for the ordinary shopper to compare the different possibilities: whereas the shopper can readily observe when one shopkeeper sells exactly the same article at a lower price than his neighbour, he is not in a position to compare the relative value of Genasprin sold at one price with Boots' Aspirin sold at a different price, because there is no common denominator of values once product differentiation takes place. There is no doubt that the consumer has widely

[1]Braithwaite and Dobbs, *Distribution of Consumable Goods* (1932). See also Chapter II, 9.

welcomed the branded articles. This welcome has been ascribed[1] to the buyers' natural sense of competition with the seller and thus to his natural pleasure at being able unreservedly to identify the article of his choice. The conflict between this view and the view stated above that the consumer shopper wants to delegate the exercise of consumers' choice is only apparent: best of all the shopper likes, in fact, to appear to be making a free choice. Thus in the case of the so-called branded goods, that is, goods with trade names, advertisement creates a preconceived idea of the value of a certain branded good like Bournville Cocoa, and the consumer, once he has been indoctrinated in the idea that Bournville Cocoa is best, is happy in the removal of the odious burden of choice and continues almost as a matter of habit, to buy Bournville, if he wants cocoa at all, or perhaps even if he wants a hot drink. Only an appreciable change in prices or conditions of sale will shift him from this preferred position.

These matters are dealt with fully in Chapters VII and VIII. The point which is relevant here is that as the standard of living has risen, consumers, or people in the spending of their incomes, have chosen to delegate to the distributive trades a wide and important range of distributive functions, and a situation has arisen in which the consumer is progressively surrendering the controlling power of demand.

Separation of wholesale and retail trading

Just as the existence of separate distributive trades, exercising particular distributive functions, is an application of the principle of the division of labour, so, within the industry, there is, in practice, a clear separation of function and organizational structure between the wholesale and retail trades and a further specialization of function between different types of retail and wholesale units.

The economics of retailing was considered in Chapters III and IV. Let us now proceed to identify the characteristics of wholesaling and to assess its economic justification.

[1]*Encyclopaedia Britannica* (11th edition), "Advertisement."

Economic case for wholesale trade

Large-scale production, if by this we mean the issue from productive units of quantities of output vastly in excess of the consumption requirements of the individual, is the general rule both here and in the United States. The economic justification of the wholesaler, which we shall use as a generic term describing all types of wholesale merchants in any marketing channel, is that he services the producers (whether of agricultural or industrial products) in the most important matter of selling their products, and he services the retailer by assembling products from a wide variety of sources and *that his intervention* can materially reduce the total cost of distribution. We say "can" because there are reasons for supposing that the current organizations of wholesale trading in this country are not as efficient as they could be: but this is a matter for the next Chapter.

Wholesale business consists primarily in selling to retailers, dealers, or distributors (who buy the goods for resale and not for their own consumption) or selling to institutional or industrial users, such as hotels, ships or railways, who purchase for business use rather than for the purpose of reselling goods in the same form[1] in contrast to retailers who typically sell to the consumers.

Are there legitimate economic grounds for the division of function between wholesalers and retailers? All distributors perform in some measure the four fundamental functions listed above but this ideal uniformity of distributive functions disappears the nearer we get to actual distributive procedures which we will investigate in the next chapter.

The middleman

The term "middleman", applied to the wholesaler, emphasizes the fact that producers at one end of the marketing channel and retailers at the other end simultaneously demand his services. The term has come, in some popular discussion,

[1]cf. U.S. Government; 16th Census; Census of Business (1940), Wholesale Trade, cf. also Board of Trade, Working Party Reports, *Cotton* (1946), 44f., and 93ff., for a description of the organization of wholesale trade in the cotton industry.

to denote something unnecessary and superabundant. There is, of course, no presumption in economics that this is the case, since the whole experience of the division of labour suggests that specialization increases efficiency. The fundamental distributive problem is to provide a bridge between centralized production and decentralized consumption, between the mass production of the modern factory and the individual homes of the consumers. This suggests two principles which together constitute a prima facie case for the economy of wholesale trading.

Principle of minimum total transactions

The first principle we may call that of Minimum Total Transactions: it is that the total number of transactions involved in marketing a given volume of goods is reduced by the interposition of trade at the wholesale level in so far as a few large shipments by manufacturers to wholesalers take the place of hundreds of small shipments which the manufacturer would otherwise make direct to retail shopkeepers. Suppose there are ten manufacturers and one hundred retailers of a particular product and that each retailer places his orders direct with the manufacturer. This would entail the dispatch of one hundred parcels by each of the ten manufacturers: a total of one thousand transactions. Each transaction involves all the detailed work of despatching an order: looking out the goods: checking with the order; invoicing; packing; collecting of accounts with all the necessary book entries; in this case one thousand times over. If, instead, the one hundred retailers sent their orders to two wholesalers, the total number of transactions would thereby be reduced, for then the ten manufacturers would each send one consignment to each of the two wholesalers (20 transactions) and the two wholesalers would each send fifty parcels to the retailers (100 transactions); a total of 120 transactions, instead of 1,000, would thus be required.[1]

In some parts of the industry, especially in connection with the small manufacturers of imitation jewellery, a greatly improved wholesale service does seem to be required. . . . There is no doubt

[1]Wholesale Textile Association, *Post-War Reconstruction* (1945) (Third and Final Report).

that . . . the enterprising wholesaler can give the small manufacturer very valuable service. He is enabled to make goods on given wholesale orders instead of speculating. More efficient planning of production is therefore possible, with avoidance of waste. There is economy in packing and despatch staff and in carriage charges, since fewer consignees are involved and individual consignments are larger. Counting-house costs are minimized, the manufacturer has a strictly limited number of large wholesale ledger accounts instead of from 50 to 100 times the number of smaller and intermittent retail customers. The manufacturer thus saves also on postage and stationery for statements and correspondence; accounts collection is simpler, cheaper and surer, and status-enquiry costs are virtually eliminated. The manufacturer also saves the heavy costs of show-rooms and travelling salesmen. Instead, he has the use of an organization which bears these costs for a number of other manufacturers simultaneously, with consequent savings to each. When it comes to competition with the foreign producer or the wrestling with a reluctant market in times of depression, the small manufacturer may be almost entirely dependent upon the enterprise of the wholesaler, and it is of great importance that he should not look to the wholesaler in vain.[1]

In more general terms, the wholesaler saves the manufacturer the cost of carrying on his books the names and details of thousands of retail stores—an important service in view of the essentially fragmentary character of most sections of the retail distributive trade. The wholesaler provides a complementary service to the retailer; the cost to any but the largest retail firms of collecting from manufacturers the wide variety of commodities which the consumer now demands would be too burdensome.

The second principle has been christened by others: it is the principle of Massed Reserves[2] or of Pooling Uncertainty.[3] The existence of the wholesaler should reduce the total amount of goods which must be held in stock to secure one of the major purposes of distribution, namely, the availability of supplies to satisfy discontinuous demands. The consumer wants to be able to buy what he wants, when he wants it, where he

[1]Working Party Reports, *Jewellery* and *Silverware.* (1946), 35.
[2]Florence, *The Logic of Industrial Organization* (1933), 17
[3]Stigler, *The Theory of Price* (1947), 331

wants it. His requirements conform to no predesigned pattern. Their definition awaits the event. Therefore, if he is to be able to obtain what he wants where he wants it all the time, just as the prudent housewife in our earlier example of the Crusoe economy found it necessary to hold supplies of goods over and above the expected average requirements of her household, so in the modern exchange economy someone must hold stocks of consumable goods if there is to be a smooth flow at every stage. By the principle of massed reserves, the total stock requirements of the community should be much less as a result of the work of the wholesalers. This may be illustrated by an arithmetical example.

The purpose of keeping a stock is to meet demands from customers which may not come at an even rate, and to bridge over delays in supply from manufacturers. Neither of these can be forecast accurately, but the more the cases, the more likely is it that the flow will be regular. Thus if a retailer has an annual turnover of £1,000 in a particular line, he might have to hold a stock worth £300 to be safe at all times. But it is not likely that he would need a stock so large as £3,000 for ten times the turnover. If, therefore, a wholesaler is ready at all times to meet sudden demands from retailers, the total stock needed will be smaller. In the example given, ten retailers acting independently would need to keep a total stock of £3,000 but with a wholesaler they might be able to keep only £100 each, and the wholesaler might be quite safe with a stock worth £1,000, thus giving a saving of £1,000 for all taken together. The larger number of retailers served, the more the saving: on the other hand, a retailer working on a really large scale has some of the advantages already, performing wholesale functions on his own account.

Holding of stocks. Division of product

Returning to our list of distributive functions on p. 75 we see that the holding of stocks and the division of the product to be sold into marketable shapes and sizes were included. This assembling of products (and the division of larger into smaller units) are perhaps the most essential services performed at the wholesale level. The conventional type of wholesaler buys and sells merchandise on his own account; he orders from the manufacturer in large lots, sometimes many months in anticipation of demand.[1] When production is complete, he accepts delivery to his own stockrooms where he assembles the product into smaller lots and stocks them until such time as the final consumer, transmitting his demands through the retailers, requires them.

U.K. textile stocks

Overall statistical data are lacking for this country but figures published by the Wholesale Textile Association give some indication of the magnitudes involved: this organization, to which all wholesalers in the textiles field belong, estimated that in 1939 the total value of stocks held in the houses of members was £20,136,105, the *cost* value of goods on hand. In addition wholesalers had book debts amounting to £19,689,305 and further commitments to the order of £17,020,655. Thus, inventories and inventory commitments amounted, at that time, to some £56,846,065. Available data are entirely lacking to construct from this total any estimate of aggregate inventory commitments for the whole of industry. It may be of some interest, however, to record that consumer expenditure on clothing constituted some ten per cent of consumer expenditure in that year.[2]

American experience

The U.S. Official Census of Business gives the total value of stocks on hand, estimated at wholesale *selling* price, as $3,872,385,000; this total represented some 7 per cent. of the value of sales during that year. This percentage value of inventories to total sales remained remarkably constant during the inter-war period, being 7.5 per cent in 1929, and 7.3 per cent in 1935 (v. Table III). Thus, wholesalers were operating on a slightly smaller inventory per dollar of sales in 1939 as compared with 1929, a period during which the total dollar volume of wholesale business diminished by 17.5 per cent.

[1]Wholesale Textile Association, *Post-War Reconstruction* (1945), 9.
[2]Cmd. 7099, *National Income and Expenditure* (April, 1947), 14.

The aggregate of commodities immobilized in the distributive pipeline is undeniably a sizeable total. It is important that these stocks or inventories should be no larger than is necessary. What are the economic issues involved in determining the right amounts, or whether they are too small or too large?

The wholesaler should perform the function of a fly-wheel or storage tank

The holding of stocks is a valuable service to the community to the extent that it enables the individual purchaser to buy what he wants when he wants it. In addition, the producer must operate at an even tempo (running full) if he is to get the economies of mass production, so that he needs the wholesaler to carry inventories which will reconcile this with the uneven tempo of consumption. The wholesaler must act as a fly-wheel or a storage tank does in the transmission of power or water to an intermittent user. On the other hand, the holding of stocks costs money to the wholesaler, and makes a demand on the real resources of the community. This is a further example of the economic problem discussed in Chapter I. If the wholesaler buys goods from the manufacturer and holds them for some time before they are bought, he has not only to provide storage facilities but also to lock up his capital, in so far as he has paid the manufacturer for the goods and has not received payment from the retailer or other bulk purchaser who will eventually buy them from him. Money is potential wealth: it is an asset which may earn income: if lent, it can earn the prevailing rate of interest. So when the wholesaler ties up his capital in the holding of stocks he requires compensation for foregoing what his capital could otherwise have earned, and the wholesaler's mark-up legitimately includes a charge on this account. (But the total charges included in the final price of the product to the consumer, on this account are likely, on the principle of Massed Reserves, to be a lesser total than it would be unless the wholesaler acted as middleman.)

The money cost from the community's point of view is that part of the wholesaler's margin which is attributable to the holding of stocks. The corresponding real cost resides in the fact that consumable goods which might otherwise be employed on sustaining productive labour are immobilized in the distributive pipeline. Up to a point these are necessary costs, i.e. costs which are incurred to secure a more than countervailing benefit.

Spread of information

The wholesaler also plays a considerable part in a second of our distributive functions: the spread of information about availability of supplies. Until recently, the economic theorist has tended to assume perfect knowledge on the part of all buyers and sellers of the character and prices of all available goods and services. This is far from the truth. The geographical separation of producers from consumers and the dual function each one of us performs, on the one hand producing and on the other hand consuming, on the one hand earning our income and on the other hand spending it, involves a situation in which it is highly improbable that the one hand will know what the other is doing—without the services of a middleman or without considerable expenditure on information services. These services are required as soon as large-scale production emerges, which requires that production be undertaken at some time before exchange can be completed.

Any increase in the knowledge of buyers concerning the whereabouts of goods they want and of sellers concerning the whereabouts of buyers who want their goods must be to their interests.

The function of spreading this information, analytically so distinct, is performed in practice in a great variety of ways by many categories of persons. All sellers are concerned to spread information as to the availability of their wares: thus manufacturers, wholesalers, retailers alike advertise their wares by a variety of means.

The part played by advertising, in the common meaning of the word, in distribution, and the total cost of advertising to the community are so great, that Chapter VII is devoted exclusively to this subject.

Suffice it here to indicate the characteristic part (outside of advertising which is also undertaken to an equal or greater extent at the manufacturing and retailing level) played by the wholesale trade in the spread of market information.

Personal contact important in trade

Wholesalers, *qua* middlemen, can establish *personal* contact with producers, manufacturers and agricultural producers, on the one hand, and with retailers on the other, which in the nature of the case would be impossible if producers sold direct to retailers. Why is this proposition self-evident? The answer is that the enormous number of transactions (see p. 80 above) which would be involved without the common denominator function of wholesaling, would make personal contact impossible or too expensive. Secondly, the wholesale house typically sends its departmental buyers periodically to its suppliers, and its travellers to its customers with the principal responsibility for ensuring the establishment and continuity of good relationship between the firm and its manufacturers on the one hand and its customers on the other. The producer is, or should be, principally occupied with production. The retailer will be principally occupied with the business of selling to the ultimate consumer. What time is left for establishing a myriad of personal contacts between the two? Yet personal contact in matters of buying and selling is essential if people are to get what they want.

It is questionable whether in the inter-war period in England, the personal contact between wholesalers and manufacturers was in all fields as efficient as it might have been. Consideration is given to this question in the following chapter.

The provision of credit facilities

The next function to be considered is the provision of credit facilities. In listing the fundamental distributive functions, we grouped these together with the function of holding stocks. It will now become clear why this grouping was chosen.

The wholesaler normally extends this function of providing credit by adding to his stock-holding service, which is a general service to all his customers, the provision of credit facilities to individual buyers. Retailers must eventually obtain from their sales the money to pay for the goods they sell; but their purchases take place before their sales. Hence no retailer can set up in business unless he invests his own or borrowed capital in his stock-in-trade. The most suitable lender of such capital is the wholesaler who, knowing the personal and trading characteristics of his customer, can make a loan by the simple means of not demanding payment until after a certain time. And this is what normally happens.

Generally speaking, the wholesaler pays prompt cash for his goods while offering liberal credit to his customers, the retailers.

U.K. wholesale textile trade

Referring again to the statistics issued by the Wholesale Textile Association, it appears that in 1938-9, the wholesaler in the field of textiles was financing distribution to the extent of approximately £34,000,000. That is to say, "if the wholesale trade in textiles had suddenly ceased to exist, the retail trade would have found it necessary to arrange a loan of the order of £34,000,000."[1]

In the United States, the Business Census for 1939 records that credit was extended on 77.5 per cent of normal wholesale business and that for some 26 per cent of this total, credit was extended for more than thirty days.

Marketable sizes and shapes

The third of the fundamental distributive functions was listed above as the assortment of commodities produced into marketable sizes and shapes.

The wholesaler typically buys goods in large lots from the manufacturer and breaks bulk for distribution to the retail trade. Thus, in the textile trade the manufacturer will supply the wholesaler with, say, 5,000 pairs of socks and the wholesaler may supply the retailer with one or several dozen pairs. The less standardized the commodity, the smaller, other things being equal, will be the unit to which bulk is broken by the wholesaler for the benefit of the retailer. Thus, while it is perfectly suitable for the wholesaler to sell dresses singly to the retailer, it may well be entirely uneconomic for the whole-

[1]Wholesale Textile Association, *Post-war Reconstruction* (1945), 10.

saler to sell so small a quantity as a single pair of socks to the retailer. In other words, there is a limit to which bulk should economically be broken and it will be suggested in the following chapter, that, in the pre-war period in this country, that limit was exceeded and instances were not uncommon of bulk being broken to such an extent that sales were uneconomic and executed at a loss. Competition cannot now be relied upon to eliminate such uneconomic practices (v. Chapter II): but agreement could be reached among traders as to what minimum quantities of goods should be supplied by wholesalers to their customers, or an ascending scale of charges could be agreed upon to discourage unit sales smaller than a certain minimum. It is most unlikely that any individual trader could afford to limit non-price competition to the extent of introducing such a scale of charges on his own. If agreement is required, some means must be found for avoiding a scale of charges determined with reference more to the monopolistic power of the associated wholesalers than the cost.

Finally, distribution involves the carriage of commodities to be sold from the point of production to the point of consumption.

In the inter-war period it was the more usual custom for the wholesaler to pay the cost of carriage on goods where the invoice value was more than a certain amount, e.g. in the textile trade, £2. The cost of carriage thus became one of the operating expenses of wholesale trade in this country. In the majority of cases, however, wholesalers did not themselves provide transportation facilities but simply paid postage or the cost of transport by rail, road or sea. In North America, on the other hand, generally speaking, it is the practice of the wholesalers not to pay carriage except within the city area in which they are situated. No hard and fast generalization for this or any other country can be made. Practice varies but in the majority of cases the wholesaler delegates the actual business of transportation to those whose main business is the provision of transportation facilities.

CHAPTER VI

WHOLESALE DISTRIBUTION IN PRACTICE

THE arguments of the previous chapter constitute an *a priori* case for the existence of a separate body of wholesale traders within distribution, and against the performance of typically wholesaling functions, as defined in the previous chapter, by either the manufacturer or the retailer. It was emphasized that the case for a separation of function was strongest where the total number of manufacturers and/or retailers was largest.

Are the wholesalers doing their job?

Whether or not this theoretical case constitutes a justification of the wholesale trade in its present form in this country depends on how far wholesalers are in practice performing the fundamental distributive functions. Let us now examine current and immediate pre-war practice with a view to answering these questions.

As the writers of the report of the Board of Trade Working Party on Lace[1] remarked: "There is hardly a single general statement of fact about (lace) distribution to which an exception cannot be found, while opinions expressed . . . about what has happened . . . have been highly conflicting."

Any treatment of the organizational aspect of wholesale trade in the United Kingdom must begin and end with the most representative of the available particular data. There is unanimity of objective opinion on the main lines of the story.

Smaller numbers employed at wholesale than at retail

The numbers employed in wholesale trade are for the most part considerably lower than those employed in retail trade in the same commodity group. Selected data derived from the 1931 census are included in the following table:

[1]Working Party Report, *Lace* (1947), 101.

TABLE II

Great Britain: Ratio of Employment in Wholesale and Retail Distribution for Selected Commodities

	A Employment (Wholesale)			B Employment (Retail)	A as precentage of B
Trade	*Male*	*Female*	*Total*	*Total*	
Sugar Confectionery	3,397	1,199	4,596	52,044	8.8
Grocery & Provision	32,331	9,980	42,311	235,561	18
Milk & Dairy Products	4,956	1,308	6,264	83,810	7·5
Meat	10,393	856	11,249	146,146	7·7
Fish & Poultry	12,017	993	13,010	38,525	33·8
Vegetables and Fruit	22,188	2,366	24,554	77,545	31·6
Tobacco	4,247	1,441	5,688	25,312	22·5
Drugs & Druggists' Sundries	6,725	4,434	11,159	50,745	22
Drysaltery, Oils & Cols.	12,179	2,335	14,514	6,945	209
Metals, Metal Goods & Tools	25,077	5,567	30,644	42,456	72
Wines, Spirits	8,657	2,068	10,725	11,193	95·8

Source: United Kingdom, *Population Census* (1931)

As these data show, while the numbers employed in distribution at the wholesale level appear to be lower for most industries than those employed at retail, there is no uniformity in the proportion of persons employed at the two levels. It is unlikely for the reasons given in Chapter that the proportion of persons engaged in distribution at the wholesale level is higher now, in 1948, than it was in 1931. No satisfactory overall estimate can however be made from the available data.

United States

In the United States in 1939, a total of 1,695,646 persons

TABLE III

United States: Comparative Summary of Wholesale Trade,[1]
1929, 1935 *and* 1939

	1939	1935	1929	*Per cent. change*	
				1935-9	1929-39
No. of Establishments	200,573	176,756	168,820	13·5	18·8
Sales	$55,265,640,000	$42,802,913,000	$66,983,024,000	29·1	–17·5
Total expenses: Amount	$5,518,456,000	$4,163,480,000	$6,025,537,000	32·5	–8·4
Per cent of sales	10.0	9·7	9·0	—	—
No. of Proprietors	133·698	97,225	90,775	37·5	47·3
No. of Employees	1,561,948	1,260,553[2]	1,510,494	23·9	3.4
Payroll: Amount	$2,624,203,000	$2,022,262,000	$2,962,774,000	29.8	1·4
Per cent of sales	4·7	4·7	4·4	—	—
Stocks on hand (end of year) Amount	$3,872,385,000	$3,106,609,000	$5,051,975,000	24·6	—23·3
Per cent of sales	7·0	7·3	7·5	—	—

[1]Source: U.S. Department of Commerce, Bureau of the Census, *Census of Business* (1940), Vol. II.

[2]Data for 1935 exclude personnel and payroll of 6,436 commission bulk stations in the petroleum trade.

were employed in wholesale business as compared with a total of more than seven million persons in full and part-time employment in retail stores in the same year.[1] The statistical pattern of wholesale trading in the United States for the years 1929, 1935 and 1939 is given in the table on page 91.

The data contained in Appendix V show that while the total dollar value of wholesale business in the United States declined between 1929 and 1939 by 17.5 per cent[2] and the total dollar value of stock on hand diminished 23 per cent, yet the number of wholesale establishments increased by nearly 19 per cent and the number of proprietors by 47 per cent. Total expenses diminished (by 8.4 per cent) but noticeably to a less extent than the diminution of turnover.

The figures indicate a tendency for wholesale businesses to do, on the average, a smaller volume of business.[3] This is an uneconomic tendency in so far as it increases the burden of overhead costs. The increase shown in Appendix V is symptomatic of this uneconomic tendency. The diminution in the total dollar volume of wholesale business is related to a number of factors such as the progressive tendency for large-scale retail trading units to buy direct from the manufacturer, thereby diminishing the total wholesale turnover, and to the artificial restraints on mortality which resulted from such institutional factors as re-sale price maintenance and the beginnings of the 'voluntary chain' in the United States in the late 'thirties and probably to the employment of financial resources accumulated during trading prior to the slump.

No representative size of business

There appear to be three distinct types of wholesaler in America, "national", "territorial" and "local" and they are known by these names. The first type, a very limited number,

[1]United States, *Census of Business* (1940).

[2]The 1935 figures are influenced by the persistence of the 1930-1 slump in trade.

[3]The United States, *Business Census*, records that the number of large wholesale establishments ("million-dollar" establishments) decreased from 6.7 per cent. of the whole in 1929 to 3.0 per cent. in 1935 with a slight rise to 3.4 per cent in 1939. Establishments with an annual turnover of less than $50,000 on the other hand increased from 30.8 per cent. of the whole in 1929 to 47.3 per cent. in 1935, returning to 43.6 per cent. in 1939.

with an annual turnover of some $150,000,000. These largest houses give employment to well over 1,000 persons. The "territorial" wholesalers operate within a defined area of within 300 to 600 miles of their headquarters; have an annual turnover of the order of $2,000,000 to $10,000,000 and employ more like 100 to 200 persons. The "local" wholesaler confines his activities to a single state. Many wholesalers operate only in New York City. Those with annual turnovers of between $1,000,000 and $2,000,000 usually employ between 50 and 100 persons and with annual turnover of less than $1,000,000 employ from 10 to 35 persons.

The same kind of hierarchy of sizes can be seen in the wholesale trade in Britain and a similar absence of a general tendency towards larger scale operation. Some of the largest wholesale houses, like Cook & Sons, operate on a nation-wide basis. These are normally big general houses, with thirty or forty departments which do not restrict themselves to a particular category of commodities. But the majority operate over a smaller field and modern tendency is towards increased specialization; that is, for wholesalers to deal in one type of commodity like hats, gloves or stockings, or household electrical equipment; though this tendency is less pronounced than it is in the United States.

General observation in the United Kingdom does not show any marked tendency for firms of one size or another to multiply within what was essentially a static industry during the inter-war period.

Wholesaling located in urban districts

Wholesale trade is a big city phenomenon. The reason for this in the case of industrial products is obvious: the aggregations of both producers and buyers are to be found in the cities. Agricultural production is, on the contrary, normally undertaken by large numbers of small producers widely scattered. For this reason, certain preliminary wholesaling functions are undertaken, in the field of farming, by assemblers: country buyers who collect produce from the farms and sell it to the nearest wholesale depot-holder. These small traders are often referred to in this country as "primary wholesalers";[1] they are middlemen operating in the chain of distribution between the producer and the main wholesaler but, since they do not normally provide storage facilities, their functions are, perhaps, more clearly identified by calling them assemblers. We shall return later in this chapter to the particular character and problems of wholesale trade in agricultural produce.

Wholesaling is, then, predominantly a big city phenomenon: in the United States, in 1940, more than one-half (52.4 per cent) of all wholesale trade was transacted by firms located in thirteen cities with a population of more than half a million persons together with the capital city in the District of Columbia. These thirteen cities contained only seventeen per cent of the country's population. The 61,732 wholesale firms located in them, however, comprised 30.8 per cent of the total number of wholesale firms. Cities with less than 50,000 inhabitants and rural areas accounted for only 19.9 per cent of wholesale sales but for 65.6 per cent of the population. Three cities taken together, New York City, Chicago and Boston accounted for one-third of the total wholesale business in the United States although they housed only 8.8 per cent of the population.[2]

Wholesaling accommodates fluctuations in the rate of production and consumption

In the previous chapter the analogy of a fly-wheel was used to explain the middleman's functions. The strain on such a mechanism is greatest when the objects it connects are moving at different speeds. Conditions in industry and trade were never in any sense normal in the inter-war period. Violent fluctuations in the level of consumer demand, both foreign and domestic, for British goods resulted in the widespread waste of industrial and agricultural productive capacity and in chronic unemployment.

[1] *Hansard*, 14 July, 1947, Minister of Food: "The primary wholesaler buys tomatoes from the growers and usually sells in bulk to a secondary wholesaler whose position is too remote or his trade too small and fluctuating to justify direct connections with growers. . . ." "The secondary wholesaler . . . buys from the primary wholesaler for re-sale in small parcels to retailers."

[2] Source: United States *Census of Business* (1940). These figures relate to the year 1940.

Pre-war and post-war instability

These dynamic changes arose from factors entirely outside of the control of wholesale traders but they had a fundamental effect on wholesale trade nevertheless. World-wide changes presented a very difficult challenge to British wholesale traders which was not effectively answered. It may be that the exacting world circumstances in this period merely underlined inherent defects in the organization of our distributive trades. After World War II, the United Nations Economic and Social Council has agreed to the avoidance of domestic economic policies which will jeopardize the maintenance of a "high and stable level" of domestic employment to which each particular member of the United Nations has committed itself. In fact, persistent post-war inflation has produced almost fevered activity in the field of industry and trade; conditions of overfull employment have prevailed.[1] Both agricultural and industrial production has so far been limited not by deficiency of demand and lack of buyers but in contrast, by bottlenecks and shortages of labour and material.[2] The wheels of production and consumption have over wide fields in this country been locked, as it were, by the operation of direct controls: allocation, consumer rationing and price administration. In these circumstances, the challenge presented to wholesale traders by this industrial fluctuation, booms and slumps of the inter-war period has not, as yet, been repeated. It is urgent to overhaul the fly-wheel mechanism, the organization of the wholesale trade, in the light of pre-war and wartime experience so that it will not be found wanting when the time comes for a return to freer trading.

Unfavourable experience in the inter-war period

We said above that the challenge of violently fluctuating levels of demand was not met by wholesale traders in the inter-war period. Reference was made in the previous chapter to the desirability of a stable level of demand. Evidence and

[1]cf. 44 above.
[2]cf. Cmd. 7046, *Economic Survey for* 1947, 20ff. and Cmd. 7344 (March, 1948), *Economic Survey for* 1948, 22ff.

opinion could be multiplied that the British wholesale trader in the inter-war period did little to cushion the impact of variations in consumer demand alike on the industrial and agricultural producer.

Wholesale trade in industrial products

As the influences bearing on wholesale trade in industrial and agricultural products differ substantially, we will deal first with the wholesaling of industrial and, later, of agricultural products.

Does branding reduce the importance of wholesale trade?

Standardization of many industrial products and the differentiation by means of branding and advertisement of one group of standardized products, for example, half-pound tins of Fry's cocoa, from another group, half-pound tins of Bourneville cocoa, and the fact that industrial products do normally perish only slowly in storage with the passage of time are factors which have exercised profound influence on the position of the wholesaler in the field of manufactured products whereas the marketing of non-processed agricultural produce has been unaffected by them.

The emergence of large-scale retailing and larger-scale manufacture has often led,[1] in such circumstances, to the by-passing of the wholesale trader. But although the large-scale manufacture of branded products has led, in many obvious instances to the manufacturer marketing his product without employing a wholesale agent, and large-scale retail firms also have by-passed the wholesaler (*v. supra*), the very various data will not fit in with any simple generalization such as that branded goods are sold direct by the manufacturer to the retailer. We are immediately confronted, should we make such

[1]For example: "In the years before the War there was evidence of a steady change in the methods of distribution in the industry. The rise of the large clothing manufacturing concerns having their own retail shops, and the increase of chain stores not owned by manufacturing concerns, together with the expansion of the volume of business done by the big retail department stores, and by certain mail order concerns, all tended to reduce the volume of the trade passing through the hands of the wholesaler on its way from the manufacturer to the retailer." Board of Trade, Working Party Report, *Heavy Clothing* (1947), 33.

a generalization, with the fact that expensive jewellery and hand-tailored garments (neither branded nor usually made by large firms) are also sold direct by the maker to the retailer or final buyer. Without census data, then, we can only trace tendencies to which there are numerous exceptions.

Valuable information on these matters is contained in the Reports of the Board of Trade Working Parties appointed after the war to report on the organization, production and distribution of a number of industries making consumers' goods other than food.

Where is the position of the wholesale trades strongest?

Wherever there is a lack of statistical data, the eventual outcome in any field of human activity appears, at first sight, to subscribe to no clear pattern. So it is with the channels of trade. On what principle has this divergence of practice emerged, some commodities being marketed at wholesale and some not? We have already noticed the effect of particular types of retail and manufacturing units on the channels of trade. Where large numbers of small manufacturers and retailers are involved, there is more likelihood that wholesaling will be conducted as a separate operation. Large-scale retailers and large-scale manufacturers tend to undertake their own wholesale activities—but they do not invariably do so. Can we now adopt another basis for our generalization and say that any particular type of commodity, as against type of producing or trading unit, has been found more or less suitable for marketing at the wholesale level?

In this respect also, there are numerous apparent inconsistencies of behaviour. Consider, for instance, the proposition that standardized articles are more likely to be marketed at wholesale than the more differentiated luxury article. Thus, the sale of mass-produced costume jewellery is normally made by the wholesaler whereas the expensive non-standardized jewellery is not. Yet immediately we encounter apparent exceptions to this general rule; for example, standard material for industrial overalls is normally sold by the converter direct to the maker-up, without a separate wholesale transaction while the more expensive fashion clothes are normally sold by the converter via the wholesaler to the maker-up.

While a final answer to these questions awaits census data for the entire field of distribution, the two Principles (80f. above) of Minimum Total Transactions and Massed Reserves are capable of more uniform application than criteria based on either the type of commodity marketed or the type of trading unit.

Thus, it will depend on the particular circumstances of production and consumption of any given article whether or not the total number of transactions will be reduced by the intervention of the wholesaler. The incidence of wholesale marketing should not be correlated with the degree of luxury character of the article without respect for the operation of those two principles because there is no high degree of correlation between the factors which determine whether economies are available by one of our two Principles (such as number of buyers and sellers) and the degree of luxury character of the product. In the above example: costume jewellery (not a fashion product but the mass-produced article) is economically marketed through the wholesaler because there are a large number of sellers (the producers) and buyers (retail stores) of this product. The same is true of fashion *clothes* but when we move on to the stage of the maker-up of fashion garments, we shall not find that the wholesaler's agency is sought because there is normally only one seller (the dressmaker) and one buyer (the potential wearer).

The Working Parties did not proceed to formulate any general principle in explanation of the particular channels of trade and their general attitude seemed to be "We do not suggest, however, that in general a wholesaling service needs to be organized, between the manufacturer and the retailer; where this does not exist *it is no doubt for a very good reason*."[1] (The italics are our own.)

Or again, in the cotton trade: the merchant converter (who buys cloth from the weaver and has it finished to his instructions by finishers working on commission) has as his three main customers the makers-up (garment manufacturers) to whom he makes 60 per cent of his sales, the wholesaler to whom he markets a further 25 per cent and other purchasers, including retailers to whom the remaining 15 per cent are sold. An

[1]Board of Trade Working Party Report, *Jewellery and Silverware* (1946), 35.

illustration of the variety of practice in the Heavy Clothing Trade is given in the following Table:

TABLE IV

United Kingdom: Percentage by Value of Made-up Clothing for Home Civilian Orders going through various channels in each section of the Industry, 1942

Section of Industry	Direct to Retailers	To Wholesalers	To Other Persons e.g., Services, Local Authorities
Proofed Clothing	38	51	11
Men's and Youths' tailored outerwear	70	22	8
Women's and maids' tailored outerwear	67	33	—
Industrial overalls and caps	49	35	16
Mens' and boys' shirts	62	36	2
Women's dresses	62	38	—
Underwear	30	70	—
Infants' wear	17	83	—
Cloth caps	35	62	3
Other made-up clothing	60	39	1
Total	58	38	4

Source: *Board of Trade Journal* (September 29, 1945).

The Working Parties gave more active consideration to the efficiency of trading methods in those industries where wholesaling was currently practised as a separate function. On this subject the various Working Parties reached surprising unanimity of opinion in the following sense:

Necessity for fuller information

(1) Primary emphasis was given to the lack of information and to the urgent need for an early consideration, on a national scale, of the distributive trades in view of their national importance:

"We feel that an inquiry into distribution in general is long overdue. A state of affairs in which manufacturers and consumers believe distributive costs to be too high, and yet are unable to confirm or to refute their opinion, is unsatisfactory. . . ."[1] or again, "On a great number of points there is need for much more accurate knowledge than is at present available, particularly on the working of all the methods of distribution and the relation between production processes and consumer demand. . . . Something like a continuing survey of distribution of a very full kind is needed by the textile industry."[2]

Or yet again "There is great lack of information on distribution. . . . The relative expansion of the distributive trades as compared with the consumer goods manufacturing industries during the 1920's and 1930's presents a serious problem which has never been thoroughly investigated. A survey of distribution would provide invaluable factual information as a basis for town planning and as a background to the subsequent Census of Distribution whose value thereby would be much enhanced."[3]

Harmful effect of distribution methods on production: (a) *Part-time working;* (b) *Excessive variety of products*

(2) The second main argument was that the behaviour of distributors impeded maximum *productive* efficiency by bringing about

(*a*) part-time working of industrial machinery owing to lack of a sufficient continuous demand;

(*b*) too great variety of types of product resulting in a failure to achieve the maximum economies of large-scale operation of plants.

The organization of retail distribution has been described in previous chapters. We are now in a position therefore to consider the impact of distributive techniques (both retail and wholesale) on productive efficiency.

[1]Board of Trade, Working Party Report, *Lace* (1947), 102f.
[2]Board of Trade, Working Party Report, *Cotton* (1946), 113.
[3]Board of Trade, Working Party Report, *Boots and Shoes* (1946), 29f.

Necessity for market research for the interpretation of demand

With respect to (*a*) the general feeling was that the development of market research and co-operative publicity[1] was required if the demand for the product of any given industry were to be stabilized and developed. It is now understood that the aggregate level of domestic demand for the aggregate output of industry and agriculture is determined to an important extent by factors outside of the control of any given industry. The British government has undertaken to maintain a high and stable level of general industrial activity—if it can. What is here in question, therefore, is the necessity for avoiding particular disequilibria between production facilities on the one hand and consumer demands on the other, in fact the fly-wheel function of the wholesaler. It is evident that when demand is continually changing, the fly-wheel function of the distributive trades must come into play if production is to accommodate changes in demand with the minimum of dislocation.

Variations in the level of demand for a particular product may arise either from variations in the timing of consumer purchases or from changes in taste. The distributive trades can minimize the impact of the former by variations in inventories and the latter by a far-sighted appreciation of changes in the pattern of consumer preference. Consideration of whether consumers' purchasing habits are in themselves unnecessarily wasteful is deferred to the final chapter.

The fly-wheel function: wholesalers' stocks cushion the impact on producers of consumers' fluctuating purchases.

Statistical data on wholesale inventories are few, but available information suggests that British wholesalers in the inter-war period did, in exceedingly trying circumstances, reduce the impact of violent changes in the level of consumer demand upon production.

Index numbers of the total value of home sales and of stocks of wholesale textile houses in this country for the period 1935-38[2] show that the large and regular seasonal variation in sales at the retail level were offset, in some measure, by seasonal

[1]Board of Trade, Working Party Report, *Lace* (1947), 109).
[2]Board of Trade, Working Party Report, *Heavy Clothing* (1947), 94ff.

changes in wholesalers' stocks. Both in men's and boys' wear and in women's and children's wear there were peaks in February or March and in September or October. Independent retailers (to whom wholesale houses chiefly sold) passed on a highly seasonal demand to wholesalers, but wholesalers by varying their stocks, passed on to the manufacturers a considerably more stable demand. The following table illustrates this fact:

TABLE V

United Kingdom: Wholesale Textiles—Index Number showing Normal Seasonal Movement in Sales and Stocks, based on 1935-8.[1]

	Jan.	Feb.	Mar.	Apl.	May	June	July	Aug.	Sept.	Oct.	Nov.	Dec.	Year
Sales	55	80	119	109	106	90	67	71	137	138	122	106	100
Stocks	95	107	106	103	99	94	101	111	107	101	95	81	100

Source: Board of Trade, Working Party Report, *Heavy Clothing* (1947), 95f., Tables XIX and XX.

Nevertheless, in spite of the equalizing effect of variations in wholesale inventories purchases from the manufacturers still remained highly unstable through industry.[2]

[1]More ample statistical data are available for the war period and illustrate the same tendency, but the issue of clothing coupons at certain periods affected the cyclical trend.

[2]See, for instance:

I. Hosiery, p. 108. "Small ordering was one of the major problems of the hosiery industry in the years before the war." . . . "Small ordering was due to many causes, the following being prominent. . . .

(*b*) Some firms trading as wholesalers had a very small annual turnover and were therefore in no position to place substantial orders

(*c*) Bad trading conditions encouraged a reluctance to carry stocks and break bulk which is the wholesaler's proper function and in many cases goods of various types were ordered in small lots at frequent intervals . . . the total costs of production and distribution were certainly higher than necessary owing to the diversification of orders."

II. Lace, p. 112. After citing the war experience of concentrated firms when output per twisthand was maintained at an "extraordinarily high" weekly level the Report goes on to say: "Experience has shown the increase in output which may be expected if reasonable production runs can be maintained. Our aim in recommending a variety of measures leading to trade expansion, e.g. market research, organized publicity, etc., is to reduce as far as possible both the fluctuations of demand to which a fashion goods industry is peculiarly susceptible and those which arise from seasonal causes. . . . It seems unlikely that completely smooth running of all firms will ever be

Discontinuity of demand results not only from changes in the timing of individual purchases but from shifts in taste. But it is extremely important to remember that the two are closely associated. It is in the fashion trades, trades in which consumers' tastes vary widely from time to time, that seasonal variations in production and employment are most serious. The cost of holding stocks consists to an important extent of losses incurred in disposing of goods which have proved unsaleable in the market for which they were originally designed.[1] Earlier buying and a bolder holding of stocks by wholesalers will result from greater certainty in market predictions.

[1]The "New Look" which came over the fashion horizon in 1947 and 1948 has presented just this problem to traders. See Harrods, Ltd., *Annual Report* (March, 1948): "As more merchandise is available, as more types and qualities of an article come on the market, a certain amount of old stock becomes unsaleable at the original price. In particular this applies to merchandise subject to the dictates of fashion. You have all heard of the 'New Look'; well, this is just a typical example of what is happening. The introduction of a new style means a necessary reduction in the price of and consequent loss on quantities of merchandise that are already in stock."

---

achieved, though if our suggestions are carried out, a greater continuity may be achieved.

Hosiery, p. 109. "Another factor which had a serious adverse effect both on manufacturing costs and on the position of hosiery workers was seasonal fluctuation of the level of ordering, which caused a considerable amount of short time working and unemployment in many hosiery factories at certain periods of the year.

III. Heavy Clothing, p. 99;

Pottery, p. 31. "The home trade demand is seasonal; seasonal variations are often exaggerated by vagaries of wealth; the seasonal swing is accentuated by variation of fashion. . . . The distributor, as the buyer, was placed in the dominant economic position with the following results: (*a*) Some manufacturers experienced late and erratic buying by distributors, (*b*) some manufacturers, who regarded themselves as having firmly established relations with their distributor customers, have had the experience of being dropped suddenly and even, upon a sudden change of business, of having their orders cancelled; (*c*) some manufacturers have been asked by some distributors to market other manufacturers' samples but at lower prices. . . .

These circumstances resulted in great variations of pressure of work in factories causing swings of under- and over- employment . . . reducing the efficiency of manufacture. We consider that this unhealthy state of affairs should not be allowed to recur and that every effort should be made to ensure greater equality of economic power between manufacturer and distributors. We do not ascribe the major share of the responsibility for variations in the flow of demand either to the manufacturers or to the distributors: we merely record that the circumstances of the trade tended to accentuate these variations and to magnify their adverse effect upon manufacturing efficiency."

In economic theory it is assumed that each individual has a scale of preferences known to himself which determines whether he will buy one or another of available commodities with a given income. The practice of advertising shows that this scale of preferences can be influenced within wide limits by influences external to the individual and to the fundamental material composition of the commodities. What the individual wants is thus seen to be a subjective concept.

Imperfect knowledge of consumer requirements at home and abroad

Over the whole of British industry, producers in the inter-war period were working in the dark about the character of consumer requirements either at home or abroad.

In the domestic field, the retailer was supposed to provide the antennae of the distributive system which sensed the impact of changes in consumer preferences through the price demand mechanism and passed it, either via the wholesaler or directly, to the producer. But there are good reasons why such a system is insufficient.

To begin with, retail distribution is inherently fragmentary in the sense that one retailer operates in and is familiar with only one portion of the national market. This applies also to most wholesalers. In the case of those whose operations are nation-wide it might be assumed that they would be able to classify the various pieces of information about the consumers' wants which come to them from the orders given by the retailers and thus provide the manufacturers with reliable information. If the assumptions of competitive theory were realized, and consumers had perfect knowledge of availability of a number of standardized products, this would be true. But, on the contrary, distribution is inherently *imperfectly* competitive.[1] In these circumstances, traders have an interest in creating artificial differences in the commodities they offer for sale in order to attract custom to themselves.

Non-price competition: Traders' demands for excessive variety for advertising purposes

The mass of traders in the inter-war period made economic production more difficult by demanding a degree of variety

[1]See Chapter II.

which was not based on what the ultimate consumer wanted so much as on their own desire to have distinctive lines for competing with each other.[1] This tendency towards "non-price" competition is an instance of the effect of economic necessity on individual action in imperfectly competitive and oligopolistic markets (See Chapter III). Its uneconomic results can only be controlled by joint action by producers, distributors and probably the government, designed to restrict excessive multiplicity of types and uneconomically small purchases by wholesalers from manufacturers and by retailers from wholesalers.

It seems clear that joint action in the matter of market research is also required. So long as production is so largely undertaken in a variety of industries by a number of small firms and so long as wholesale trade also is conducted on a small-scale basis particular firms will be unable and unwilling to make extensive investigations into actual and potential consumer demands. Moreover, great economies can be achieved by centralizing the provision of market intelligence. But a situation in which the majority of producers and traders are working in the dark, ignorant of the facts of the market in which they are operating, is extremely wasteful both from the community's point of view and from that of the individual. The breakdown of intelligence occurs at all levels of distribution: the manufacturer produces with the wholesaler and/or retailer in mind but the retailer's technical knowledge of his wares is often extremely limited and the customer more often than not buys completely in the dark. Again retailers'

[1]cf. Board of Trade, Working Party Report, *Cotton* (1946), 104. Also Hosiery (1946), 108f. "25 per cent of manufacturers replying to the Working Party's questionnaire intended to make smaller ranges of goods than pre-war, and 34 per cent, intended to restrict the number of styles they offered in each of the ranges. It will be difficult however (the report adds) for most individual manufacturers to resist the pressure for an excessive number of new lines from the distributive trade which will inevitably tend to occur when the selling position weakens. We do not intend this remark as a general criticism of either manufacturers or distributors, but rather as relating to the effect of *economic necessity on individual action*. (The italics are our own.) . . . In their efforts to increase their business and show a profit, distributors, both wholesale and retail, made continual efforts to obtain 'something different', with the result that manufacturers were continually being asked for new styles, patterns and colours . . . total costs of production and distribution were certainly higher than necessary owing to the diversification of orders."

and/or wholesalers' orders to manufacturers are not a perfect mirror of consumers' preferences because they are in a large measure determined by the trader's own peculiar position in an imperfectly competitive market.

Consumer research in the United States

In the United States the basis of salesmanship is rather different in industries subject to fashion or where design of the commodity is of importance—which is over a wide field. There[1] "elaborate and enterprising consumer research is undertaken by experts on behalf of the Manufacturers' Association which also arranges for publicity experts to build up new types of design and new fashions in advance of the actual production of goods . . . the whole method with its large financial commitment, both makes the manufacturer keenly aware of the importance of design and causes him to appreciate the value of the longer term; when his market is going well he concentrates on the efficiency of his production and distribution of established lines to catch up with the demand; when there is a slump, he seeks to find out why his old lines are losing power with the public and to fix upon a good line to build up for the future. His very methods make him think and plan for a longer term instead of living from hand to mouth and simply continuing to make in hope the goods which commanded the interest of his customer in the last boom several years ago. . . ." The retailers will not, any longer, play the dominating part and "the industry should feel great relief from the increased steadiness and virility of the market which the new methods should be able to secure."

Will the forces of competition eliminate inefficient businesses and business methods?

It might be argued that if the wholesaler was not in fact adequately performing his economic function then he would by competitive processes and the working of the profit motive be eliminated in so far as neither manufacturers nor retailers would find it worth their while to employ him as middleman but

[1]cf. Board of Trade, Working Party Report, *Jewellery and Silverware* (1946), 32ff.

would, instead, trade directly with one another providing their own wholesaling facilities. It has been seen that this did, to a certain extent, occur: there was a tendency for large-scale retail firms to buy direct from the manufacturers and for large-scale producers to endeavour to control their own retail market by branding, advertisement, and direct sales to retailers. But in the field of small production and retail units the wholesaler, in this country, lost little ground.

It will be seen in Chapter VII on Advertising that in many cases the wholesalers attempted to maintain their position by means of advertising and resale price maintenance. In some cases, manufacturers chose to sell direct to large retailers. By and large, although the wholesale trade did not expand in spite of an increasing level of economic activity, no dramatic changes took place in the organization of wholesaling or in trading methods in Great Britain. In the general industrial and commercial lethargy which characterized the inter-war period in this country, the deterioration of efficiency was not met by new forms of competition at the wholesale level so much as by a resort to security measures such as Trade Association and resale price maintenance. Many wholesalers possessed large pre-slump reserves which enabled them to carry on. Then war froze the organizational pattern, and guaranteed margins as a result of government price administration guaranteed at the same time the continued existence even of the inefficient. There has been little indication, so far, of any change.

American experience: evolution of the voluntary chain

In the United States, still, unlike this country, a rapidly expanding economy, a similar situation produced a dramatic competitive reaction which is of interest. In the inter-war period, the fierce competition of the chain stores was a direct threat to the wholesale trade. It was as a result of initial intensive price competition that the chain stores originally drove through consumers' resistance and gained a footing: they could survive as large-scale retail units or not at all and their policy of intensive price competition was made possible by an imaginative buying policy based on side-stepping the wholesalers and giving bulk orders directly to the manufacturers.

The manufacturers responded. What they wanted (and what the wholesale trade was not giving them) were large orders ahead of time. These parallel economic interests constituted a grave threat to the American wholesaler.

It will be seen from Table III that during the decade 1930-1940, (while the total population of the United States increased slightly less than 7.2 per cent.,) the total number of persons engaged on wholesale distribution increased by only 5.9 per cent (1929-39), while the total dollar volume of wholesale business diminished by 17.5 per cent (1929-39). The index of wholesale prices shows a decline from 86.4 to 77.1 (1926 base) for the same period. In spite of the 17.5 per cent decrease in the total value of wholesale business the number of establishments increased from 169,000 (1929) to 200,000 (1939) and the payroll diminished from $2,962,774,000 (1929) to $2,624,203,000 (1939). These figures show a tendency for the average size of unit to diminish. The tendency for the average size of wholesale businesses to diminish, in the United States, during the 1930s is a striking contrast to the reverse tendency at the retail level for the average size shop to increase.

As an illustration of the self-generating character of monopoly and also of the organizational mobility of American economic life, the development of the Voluntary Chain in the United States is striking.

What is the Voluntary Chain?

The wholesalers, being confronted with the challenge of direct purchase by the chain stores from the manufacturers, have evolved a form of organization which has been cited as a decided challenge, in its turn, to the competition of the chains. The system has, as its primary object, the placing of the independent retailer in a position successfully to compete with the chain stores. In effect, under the voluntary chain system, the wholesaler of a particular type of goods acts for a group (voluntary chain) of retailers in exactly the same manner as the headquarters of the chain store acts for its branches.

Mr. W. T. Caves reports as follows on what he saw of the voluntary chains in the United States during his visit this spring (1947).

"Under agreements," he writes,[1] "independent retailers tie themselves to a wholesale house, undertaking to buy all (or in some cases "as much as possible") from that house. Keener prices are obtained. Service is also provided in the way of sales promotion, advice on layout, display, advertising, merchandising and financial control, etc., for which a charge of from £100 per annum upwards is made. One warehouse in the United States operates a group of some 2,000 retailers on these lines. A model plan ensures stock is kept up to a proper level by means of check lists on which the trader marks off goods sold and orders weekly. No salesmen call, but a staff of experts are employed to make frequent visits, advising on all aspects of retail management.

Evidence that the voluntary chain system arrested the expansion of business by the chain stores

"Wholesalers who operate voluntary chains assert that if they had not done so they would eventually have had to close their doors as 'the chain stores were running them out of business.' They take the view that the wholesaler did not keep himself in line with modern trends and, in particular, did not keep his customer in mind. By the operation of voluntary chains which are, in effect, tied accounts, the wholesaler has been able to safeguard the independent retailer and prevented his business from being bought over by the chains. Similarly, the provision in the franchise which requires the retailer to give the wholesaler the first refusal when he desires to sell, assures that the business will not fall into the hands of the chains. When a retailer, in fact, decides to sell out, the business is bought by the wholesaler who then proceeds to find a worthy successor whom, if necessary, he will finance until such time as he is firmly established."

Voluntary Chains are monopolistic in character but are economic where they lead to an improvement in the technique of retail distribution

There seems to be no doubt that the system of "voluntary chains" will grow in America, in spite of their restrictive

[1] *The Drapers' Record*, March 15, 1947.

character, because they appear to be successfully combating the competition of the chains. They have discovered means of increasing the survival value of the small-scale retailer and the small-scale wholesaler in the face of competition from the chains.

From the analysis of Chapters II and III it would appear that the small-scale independent retailer has a definite and particular function and that it is therefore undesirable from the economic and special point of view that this type of retail unit should be eliminated. If so, some such system as the voluntary chain which enables this type of retail unit to survive, *in so far as it does so by making him more efficient*, is valuable.

It appears that the business methods of the small-scale retailer have in many details improved as a result of the influence of the voluntary chains and there is another important respect in which these organizational developments appear to be economic: "The 'voluntary chain' system is worked in conjunction with more 'selective distribution'; the two systems appear to be complementary one to the other and result in the wholesaler carrying a less extensive range of goods than he did when he traded on the old lines of buying from all and sundry manufacturers."[1]

Selective distribution

"Selective distribution" is a term which has recently come into widespread use in wholesaling circles in the United States and has made its appearance here. It is "a method of merchandizing by which the producer, instead of selling his product to all who are competent to handle it, selects a certain adequate but limited number of outlets and confines his distribution to these outlets."[2] According to Mr. Flint Garrison, the system was devised "because everybody in the wholesale trade was trying to sell the same thing to the same customers and, in doing so, received no co-operation from either manufacturer or retailer," besides involving waste in duplication of transactions which it is hoped by means of wholesaling to minimize.

[1]Wholesale Textile Association, *Secretary's Report on Delegation to America and Canada* (1947).

[2]Mr. Flint Garrison, Director U.S. Wholesale Dry Goods Institute.

Selective distribution entailed the engagement on the part of the manufacturer to limit the sale of his products to a limited number of wholesalers in different parts of the country and, on the part of the wholesaler, to confine himself to a selection of distinctive products and definitely relate himself to certain sources of supply."

In so far as selective distribution denotes a tendency towards greater concentration, by any given firm at the wholesale level, on a given commodity group, it should be welcomed. Appreciable economies can be secured from handling less varied aggregates of commodities through more thorough knowledge of the particular goods and of the producers and retailers in the particular field.

These two organizational developments in the United States, the "voluntary chain" and "selective distribution," are closely associated and taken together they present a striking contrast to British experience.

Criticism of British pre-war practice

Criticism of wholesale business in the United Kingdom has been widespread on the following counts: many wholesalers in the inter-war period were not performing two important bona fide economic functions of the wholesaler, namely, carrying stocks[1] and breaking bulk, but were tending to concentrate too greatly on the function of supplying credit to retailers and on the speculative possibilities which always attend buying for re-sale. Where this was so wholesalers were working, as we have said, on the back of the manufacturers. Manufacturers were presented not with a fifty-week planned order but with a multitude of fragmentary orders on the basis of a range of "samples". Armed with these samples, several wholesalers would send travellers to visit each tiny shop and make a further series of repeat orders on the basis of their sales. Working on a margin as high as 15 per cent to 20 per cent, large numbers of wholesalers on the outbreak of war were finding it difficult to make their business pay.

The two grave disadvantages of such a system are, first,

[1]Board of Trade, Working Party Report, *Cotton* (1946), 103.

that wholesale business conducted on this basis fails to fulfil the function of wholesaling, namely, lessening the impact of discontinuity of demand on the producer who requires a constant rate of production for efficiency; secondly, that the cost of wholesale business, in such circumstances, is itself unnecessarily high. The economies which result from large-scale production or distribution can result just as easily from expansion in the total value of sales *of a particular category of commodity* as from an increase in the total value of sales of all commodities. The first can be achieved without the second where the wholesaler reduces the number of lines in which he does business.

Report of Post-War Reconstruction Committee of the Wholesale Textile Association

The Post-war Reconstruction Committee of the Wholesale Textile Association reports that manufacturers complained generally of their treatment by wholesalers, relationships were strained and they were inclined to seek other classes of customers, namely, the retailers or large-scale final buyers. It appears that this breakdown of the wholesaling function arose and was associated with the prevalent custom of individual wholesale houses of delegating "most matters concerned with the purchase of supplies to their departmental buyers upon whom, therefore, rested the responsibility of ensuring the establishment and continuity of good relationship between the firm and its manufacturers. Buyers, naturally, tended to regard the well-being of their department as their primary consideration, which taking the short view was probably right, but which for a long-term policy must inevitably have adverse results . . . no machinery existed whereby manufacturers could express their views and thoughts to the principals of the firm without finding themselves in disfavour with the buyer. There is no doubt that many manufacturers, both large and small, were restrained from discussing their problems with the principals of wholesale houses by the knowledge that sooner or later they might lose the account." This is clearly not an insuperable difficulty. The W.T.A. suggests that the establishment of joint standing committees composed of representatives of manufacturers and wholesalers should meet regularly to discuss matters affecting the relationship of buyer and seller.

On the selling side too, it appears that certain organizational defects prevented the highest degree of mutual accord from being established, in certain fields, between wholesaler and retailer. Such instances seem to occur more frequently where there has been a lesser degree of specialization both as regards the range of goods stocked and the prices at which those goods are offered by the wholesaler. Reference has already been made to a new form of organization; the voluntary chain in existence in the United States and under active discussion in this country, may present a partial solution.

Neither voluntary chains nor selective distribution are in this country more than subjects of discussion at the present time. But there is an increasing body of opinion in wholesale circles which favours the increased specialization that is taking place, and there is an increasing body of opinion which condemns a system of distribution that magnifies rather than reduces the fluctuations of consumer demand and thus increases rather than reduces the waste occasioned by producers working at under-capacity because of periodic fluctuations in the demand for their product.

The direct limitation of competition is as we have seen a striking feature of the American solution to these problems. There is a strong feeling, the result to a large extent of nineteenth century economic theory, but for which there are admirable grounds when properly stated and understood, that forms of organization which limit competition are prima facie suspect. If this argument is formulated positively as the proposition that a competitive system tends by the pricing mechanism to secure the sale of output at the lowest possible prices and towards the elimination of the least efficient, it cannot be gainsaid. But in Chapter III we show that distribution is inherently non-competitive in the full sense of the word as used in the above statement.

How far should wholesaling be competitive?

The present position is then that the ordinary man who has no time to study economics has received years, nay decades of indoctrination, in the theory that competition is a virtue (which it is), but the definition of competition has not been revealed to him. It cannot be deduced from the fact that competition is a virtue that any of the characteristics of a state of competition, as for instance, absence of restrictive agreements between buyers and sellers, taken out of conjunction with all the other characteristics is, in itself, virtuous. That would be like arguing that since a varied diet is conducive to good health, the diabetic should be given sugar which is a constituent of a varied diet. So it may be that some of the defects of our present system of wholesale distribution can only be remedied by limitations of competition. The public however, would be well advised to consider carefully the possible virtues of any such schemes which the wholesale trade may itself devise in this post-war period before condemning them as monopolistic, but it should note their inherently monopolistic character and take appropriate means of securing the public interest by proscribing restrictive business practices.[1] The alternative is some form of state operation of wholesale marketing by public utility corporations.[2] Even if this last solution were preferred, it would be unwise to embark on such a plan until considerably fuller information on these trades, such as can only result from the census of distribution, becomes available.

In the field of industrial products, as we have seen, there are strong forces making for the elimination of the middleman: the increased concentration of economic power both at wholesale and retail, which is based on large-scale production and large-scale retailing, has given rise to a situation in which the manufacturer of branded and highly advertised goods strives to become independent of intermediate brokers whereas the large-scale retailer for reasons given in Chapter IV has chosen to buy direct from the manufacturer.

No hard and fast generalizations can be made: the manufacturer of highly advertised branded goods, who frequently markets a part of his output direct to the large retailer or large institutional consumers, often simultaneously uses the agency

[1]See Chapter IX.

[2]Ministry of Agriculture and Fisheries, Economic Series 48 (1947), *Report of the Committee appointed to review the working of the Agricultural Marketing Acts* ("Lucas Report"), 55.

of the wholesaler for contact with the numerous smaller shops to which he also sells. The wholesaler most commonly retains his position in the sale of bulk goods, produced on a small or moderate scale, neither proprietary nor branded articles (in the sale of which advertisement therefore plays little part). It is in these circumstances that the principles of wholesaling are likely to operate most effectively.

There are circumstances in which the interposition of more than one middleman can be justified by reference to the operation of the Principles of Minimum Total Transactions and Massed Reserves and we find that in practice, wholesale functions have been sub-divided.[1]

Importance of wholesale trade in farm produce

Market conditions likely to occasion a sub-division of the wholesale function, while not absent in the field of industrial products,[2] are most frequently found in the sale of farm produce.[3]

Wholesale trade likely to be most important where

(1) *Imperfect knowledge of availabilities on part of large numbers of producers and retailers*

These conditions may, perhaps, be listed as follows:

(1) Knowledge of market availabilities may be so inadequate among large numbers of small producers and large numbers of small retail outlets, that a specialization of function occurs between those who are engaged in finding out and co-ordinating sources of supply and those who are engaged in finding out and co-ordinating retail outlets and this specialization of function, occasioning as it does the interposition of two middlemen,

[1]Braithwaite and Dobbs, The Distribution of Consumable Goods (1932), 143: "Among the names most commonly applied to the performers of some part or other of the wholesale function we find those of broker, commission house, commission salesman, manufacturer's agent, purchasing agent, commission buyer, higgler and jobber. A division can be made between those who buy the goods outright and those who act solely as agents for producers or merchants."

[2]cf. Working Party Report, *Cotton* (1947) for function of merchant converter.

[3]Minister of Agriculture and Fisheries, Economic Series No. 48 (1947), *Report of the Committee appointed to review the working of the Agricultural Marketing Acts.*

the assembling wholesaler and the distributing wholesaler, between the producer and the retailer, is economic from consumers' point of view as a legitimate application of the division of labour and also as a demonstration of the two principles of wholesaling.

British agriculture in the inter-war period consisted, and still does consist, of "a mass of small-scale, highly individualistic producers, each of whom, whether from choice or through lack of machinery for organization, worked on his own. There were and still are, some 446,000 farms in Great Britain, 346,000 of which comprise less than 100 acres each, 276,000 less than 50 acres".[1] The individual farmers, widely scattered and without any adequate system of market intelligence, handed over the produce of their farms to local assemblers who collected it from the individual farms (or the importer in the case of imported produce) and transported it to the nearest local wholesale market. There the produce was purchased by the distributing wholesaler who normally undertook the final work of distribution, to the retailer.[2]

(2) *The perishable character of goods to be marketed puts a premium on speedy exchange.*

(2) The perishability of farm produce involved the necessity for completing market processes with the utmost speed. In proportion as goods are perishable they are less suitable for sale by description or by sample and the town wholesaler busy with the business of selling to retailers may then find it well worth his while, rather than leave his business, to employ an agent to go round the farms and buy the kind of produce he requires after inspection: the agent buys the goods from the producer for immediate resale and frequently does not himself handle them; the town wholesaler to whom he sells or the farmer normally arranges for transport and/or storage, which he endeavours to reduce to a minimum. The marketing of potatoes and other vegetables, fruit, eggs and poultry are of this kind. Braithwaite and Dobbs[3] note that the economic

[1]Ministry of Agriculture and Fisheries, Economic Series No. 48 (1947), pp. 4 and 5.

[2]Braithwaite and Dobbs, id., 142f.

[3]Braithwaite and Dobbs, id., 145.

functions performed by the commission salesman and buyer are substantially the same, the main difference being the manner of payment: the commission agent is normally paid a certain percentage on the value of the transaction he effects whereas the merchant assembler buys the goods outright and his remuneration is determined by his success in gauging the market. There is no doubt that the intervention of a second intermediary expedites the marketing process in these circumstances.

(3) *Specialized credit facilities are required*

(3) Specialization in the provision of credit facilities at wholesale has been given[1] as an occasion for an extra middleman. In certain trades the large wholesaler has found it more convenient to delegate the provision of credit facilities to local wholesalers who are intimately familiar with their customer's financial reputation. While this provides a possibility of economic sub-division of wholesale functions, practical reasons were given earlier in this chapter for supposing that this tendency has been carried too far. Where the wholesaler specializes in the provision of credit facilities to small buyers he tends to do so at the expense of other wholesale responsibilities—so that this tendency would appear to be a symptom not so much of specialization as of the neglect by a certain type of trader of functions which it is in the interests of the community that he should simultaneously perform. Such a division of function, although uneconomic, can arise from the combination of imperfect competition—leading to excessive non-price competition—and bad trade.

(4) *The process of grading and sorting requires particular experience*

(4) Where the process of grading and sorting requires particular knowledge and experience or is particularly arduous, there may be occasion for sub-division of the wholesale function. Farm produce leaves the farm, too often, in a soiled condition; soil must be removed and the produce assorted in a manner which is suitable for purchase and sale; potatoes are cleaned and sorted; carrots are sorted and bunched, and so on. Where there is already a sub-division of function and a first- and second-hand buyer from the farm, the first-hand buyer would

[1]Braithwaite and Dobbs, id., 146.

probably perform this function. Here, as everywhere in the field of marketing, there is great diversity of practice. An alternative means of securing the same end would be standardized grading and packing. Despite efforts of the Ministry of Agriculture and Fisheries through the "National Mark" movement and in other ways, standardized grading and packing of farm produce was the exception before the war. Lack of standardization set an automatic limit to restrictive practices such as resale price maintenance, but, on the other hand, it prevented the economy in distribution costs which results from the fact that a product which is graded and packed can be sent direct from the packing centre to the retailer without intermediary inspection or handling.

Criticism of trading methods in the inter-war period

The verdict of independent opinion seems to be that "amongst the many and complex factors which were responsible for the almost continuously depressed position of British agriculture in the period between the two world wars, there was one which stood out for all to see . . . the channels of disposal were to a large extent antiquated, circuitous and excessively costly.[1]"

The wholesale distribution of agricultural produce manifested the same uneconomic tendencies as in the field of manufacture: in the main, the wholesaler was failing to discharge his flywheel function of insulating the farmer from the full impact of variations in the level of demand. The wholesale distribution of agricultural produce was frequently organized in relatively small-scale units with inadequate storage facilities. One of the main weaknesses before the war in the marketing of agricultural produce was the lack of proper provision for storage.[2]

Few, however, would fail to admit that British agriculture was subject to a number of disturbing influences pre-war of such magnitude that the marketing methods of particular traders, however efficient from the technical point of view

[1]Ministry of Agriculture and Fisheries, Economic Series No. 48 (1947) 6.

[2]In the marketing of agricultural produce the holding of stocks can and should play an important part in levelling out seasonal and other short term fluctuations for commodities such as eggs, potatoes or even meat and for the non-perishable commodities like wheat and other grains, variations in ihventories may even provide the basis for longer-term stability of prices

could not have accommodated them sufficiently to maintain a high and stable level of demand for the farmer's produce.

Agricultural Marketing Acts, 1931-3

In these circumstances, whereas the free play of market forces was permitted, without government intervention to determine both the channels and costs of distribution of non-food consumers' goods in pre-war Britain, the emergence in the field of agriculture of problems comparable to those already described gave rise to state intervention after 1931, through the Agricultural Marketing Acts. Distribution problems in the field of agriculture, though the same in kind as those already described, were intensified as a result first of the more intensive competition of imports and, secondly, by the even more widespread ignorance of market conditions of the agricultural as compared with the industrial producer.

Wherever agricultural production is undertaken by a large number of small producers, the economic marketing of their produce has presented characteristic problems which have been met, in many countries, by voluntary co-operative selling by the farmers. The British farmer's traditional attitude to marketing was, pre-war, that it was none of his business.

In these circumstances, the persistence of trade depression in 1930-1 and the threat of farmers' insolvency, fear that agricultural workers might be thrown out of employment and swell the inflated total of domestic unemployment, together with the fear that increased imports of agricultural produce would increase the disequilibrium in the balance of payments, led the Government to intervene.

The form of intervention adopted was that of enabling Acts: under the Agricultural Marketing Acts, 1931-3,[1] producers of

[1] *Agricultural Marketing Act*, 1931, 21 and 22 Geo. 5, Ch. 42; *Agricultural Marketing Act*, 1933, 23 and 24 Geo. 5, Ch. 31; *Agricultural Marketing No. 2 Act*, 1933, 24 Geo. 5, Ch. 1. The first Act aimed primarily at a reform of marketing; producers were to submit schemes which, if approved by the government and the majority of farmers, were to become legally enforceable. Previous voluntary attempts at co-operative selling by farmers had broken down. The second Act linked marketing reorganization with restriction of imports, since the Ottawa agreements and the transition to Protection had been made in the interval. It also extended the provisions which enabled farmers to increase the prices they received. The third Act made no changes of major importance.

any agricultural product[1] could, upon a two-thirds majority-vote, both by number and by productive capacity, form a Producer Board which could "make regulations governing the sale of the commodity at any stage between producer and consumer. They could limit the amount of the product that could be offered for sale and they could use any method they liked for the sharing among members of the whole income derived from the sale of the product. In short, they were given the powers of a statutory and inviolable monopoly."[2] The aim of these provisions was to prevent widespread weak selling by farmers in times of bad trade as a result of lack of information on any but the most local market conditions, insufficient financial resources to tide the farmer over a bad year and the difficulty, amounting in the short run to an impossibility, of varying his supplies either by restricting production or storage, facilities for which were normally very limited.

The remarkable truth is that, by the outbreak of war, schemes for only five commodities had been brought into operation under these Acts; they were for hops, milk, potatoes, pigs and bacon respectively. Schemes for sugar, fruit, livestock, eggs and poultry had been drafted but not accepted. Where formerly apathy, or even hostility, to the Acts existed, there is nowadays an eager desire not only to secure as soon as possible the full resumption of marketing schemes now in suspense or partial operation, but also to promote additional schemes.[3] When the dangerously generous terms of the enabling Act are considered it is dramatic testimony to the pre-war individualism of the British farmer that so little use, comparatively speaking, was made of the provisions. The explanation brought forward

[1]An "agricultural product" was defined in the 1931 Act as any product of agriculture or horticulture and any article of food or drink wholly or partly manufactured or derived from any such product, and fleeces and the skins of animals.

[2]Ministry of Agriculture and Fisheries, *Economic Series* 48 (1947), 6.

[3]Ministry of Agriculture and Fisheries, *Economic Series* 48 (1947), 53: "We gathered from the evidence presented to us by the National Farmers' Unions that producers' representatives consider that there is a sound case for a marketing scheme for virtually every product of British agriculture, with the exception of sugar beet. . . . It would appear that where formerly apathy, or even hostility, to the Acts existed, there is nowadays an eager desire not only to secure as soon as possible the full resumption of marketing schemes now in suspense or partial operation, but also to promote additional schemes."

by the Lucas Committee is "Farmers proved to be less willing to organize self-help in the field of marketing than to accept government subsidy."[1] "In the immediate pre-war period, there was hardly a major product of British agriculture that was not the subject of a subsidy."

Pre-war techniques of agricultural marketing provide no solution for post-war problems

Experience under the Agricultural Marketing Acts is, nevertheless, of considerable importance to us at this moment. The farmers, accustomed to extensive government wartime controls, appear to have lost their aversion to the techniques of control provided for in the pre-war Acts and now that the question of the abandonment of wartime controls is under active discussion the National Farmers' Union are strongly in favour of a return to and extension of the system under the Agricultural Marketing Acts for almost every product of British agriculture. It is therefore of some importance that the public should realize the issues involved:

(*a*) The marketing schemes were based on the organized restriction of farmers' output with a view to maintaining prices: a simple application of the principles of monopoly pricing. Consent of the distributors, by this time fairly powerfully organized, was necessary to the working of the scheme and was secured by the guarantee of minimum prices and margins both wholesale and retail: with resale price maintenance in the field of farm produce, diminished volume of sales would have led to reduced profits for traders in the absence of increased margins: the tendency was thus for distributors' margins to be raised. Only the final consumer suffered by paying higher prices for his food.

(*b*) No reorganization of the admittedly antiquated channels of distribution was undertaken. No investigation of the possibility of reducing marketing costs was undertaken by the Boards who uniformly adopted the policy of financing increased producers' prices by raising retail prices. What inducement had producers to incur the opposition of distributors in this matter? Consumers' representatives carried little weight in opposition to organized producers' and distributors' interests. How much more dangerous such a combination would be under full

[1]Ministry of Agriculture and Fisheries, *Economic Series* 48 (1947), 12.

employment is suggested by the Lucas Committee.[1] "The danger was ever present that a bargain might be struck" (between sellers organized in Producer Marketing Boards and organized distributors) "which reflected not so much the relative bargaining strengths of the organized sellers and buyers as the facility with which the two parties could combine and exploit the consumers."

There is no presumption that *laisser-faire* in the field of distribution which is inherently imperfectly competitive and oligopolistic will result in the development of the most efficient techniques of wholesale distribution. We are confronted with contrasting developments: in some cases the sub-division of the wholesaling function has led to an increase in the number of middlemen; in others the elimination of wholesalers from the distributive chain has taken place. It is the argument of these chapters that neither result can be presumed to be desirable from the national point of view simply because it was, at some stage, profitable and therefore took place. In general, it appears that where more than two distributors are concerned, in addition to the producers, a legitimate reason can be found in that they, the producers, are less well organized than is usual, or else in some other special feature which necessitates more than the average amount of selling services and selling effort. Where the number of middlemen is reduced below the normal figure, the commonest explanation is that either the producer or the retailer works on such a large scale that it is economical to dispense altogether with the wholesaler's services.[2] The numerous cases in which the manufacturer sells direct to the consumer primarily because he finds this a convenient means of pushing the sale of his goods against those of his competitors indicates the possibility of changes in the channels of trade which may well be uneconomic from the national point of view.

Laisser-faire, then, does not provide a complete answer, but experiments at control have, up to date, proved disappointing from the point of view of reducing the cost by improving the efficiency of wholesale distribution. It is in these circumstances that its nationalization is proposed.

[1]Ministry of Agriculture and Fisheries, *Economic Series No.* 48 (1947), 6.
[2]cf. Braithwaite and Dobbs, *Distribution of Consumable Goods* (1932), 117.

CHAPTER VII

ADVERTISING

Advertising is one of the forms of non-price competition which naturally result from conditions of oligopoly

IN Chapter III it was stated that the seller could increase his sales by extra selling costs which induced people to buy from him who would not be attracted by price reductions. It was also shown how the conditions of an imperfect market gave rise to conditions of oligopoly in which producers and sellers had an eye to their competitors' probable reactions in determining their own sales policies. In such circumstances there is a tendency to restrain price competition and turn to other methods of attracting consumer interest and thereby of selling goods. Advertising is a firmly established and effective instrument of this kind.

Expenditure on advertising

The whole question of advertising has recently come to the forefront of public discussion. A variety of circumstances has produced this result. Published estimates of the total cost of advertising,[1] which appears to have been running at the rate of some £89 million a year in the United Kingdom before the war, shocked the public from the angle of social accounting. Was the public right in spending some 2.2 per cent of the national income (a sum equivalent to some 70 per cent of the income of all schools, and nearly nine times the expenditure on

[1]Bishop, *The Economics of Advertising* (1944), 54, quotes the *Statistical Review's* (July, 1943) estimate of £125 million for 1935 and *The Economist's* (Feb. 20, 1947) estimate of £85 million for 1935. Bishop himself (Id. 63), estimates the annual expenditure on advertising 1935-8, in Great Britain at £80,500,000 or approximately 2 per cent of the national income. Equivalent expenditures in the United States in 1935 were about 3 per cent of the national income, $1,700,000,000 (£320,000,000 converted at $4.86 to the £1). (Estimate made by the Graduate School of Business Administration at Harvard University and quoted by Borden, *Economic Effects of Advertising*, 54).

new books)?[1] This question was asked at a time when the whole question of distribution costs and techniques was in the air. The suspicion arose that distribution costs (paid for by the consumer, in the price he paid for the product) were needlessly multiplied by imperfect competition among producers and sellers. Advertising was regarded by some as "typical of these expenditures"[2] and by all as a principal constituent item; it thus came in for a considerable degree of attention. So much was this so, that Sir Stafford Cripps, in his austerity proposals to meet Britain's accelerating economic crisis, August, 1947, included the taxation of advertising expenditure in order, he said, to bring about a reduction in advertising expenditure.[3]

The value of advertising to the community

The question whether the community gets its money's worth from national outlay on advertising has sometimes been put in a way which requires the answer no! This has been done by making a vigorous distinction between two types of advertising: one white and one black; one economic and the other wasteful. Little justification has been given of this dichotomy though it is or should be of the greatest practical importance. The goodness and badness of these two types of advertising, informative and persuasive, is implied to be self-evident, following necessarily from the definitions.

Constructive and combative advertising: persuasive and informative

Marshall[4] makes the same distinction, using the terms "constructive" and "combative" advertising, the purpose of the former being "to draw the attention of people to opportunities for buying and selling, of which they may be willing to avail themselves and the latter designed by one manufacturer to draw custom away from another." Attempts have even been

[1]National Institute of Economic and Social Research, Kaldor and Silverman, *A Statistical Analysis of Advertising Expenditure*, (1948), 6.

[2]Chamberlin, *Theory of Monopolistic Competition*,[3] (1938), 118.

[3]The tax proposal was rejected after a promise had been secured from the Federation of British Industries and representative Associations of traders to secure a reduction in advertising expenditure by voluntary means.

[4]Marshall, *Industry and Trade*, 305. cf. also Lever, *Advertising and Economic Theory*, (1947) 47ff.

made to estimate what proportion of the total expenditure is informative in contrast to persuasive. For example, the National Institute of Economic and Social Research estimates that, of a total expenditure on advertising in this country in 1935 of £90 million more than half, some £50 million, was primarily persuasive.[1] The Economist adds, "£50 million is a large sum to spend on persuasion."

Is the distinction coherent?

It is extremely doubtful whether this simple approach is sound or useful.

The difficulty experienced in classifying actual advertising expenditure in this way is not primarily the admitted crudity of the statistical data but it is philosophical; the notions of informative and persuasive advertising contain an inherent contradiction; it is the implication that there is some objective criterion of human want as distinct from the current state of human preference. Suppose Mr. A, after reading the advertisements for Smoothflesh Soapless Shaving Soap, stops buying Freshface Foam, which he previously used, and transfers his custom to Smoothflesh. It requires that we should determine whether this change in the A's preference for a particular brand of soap has resulted: (1) from the fact that the advertisement of Smoothflesh merely made him aware of its availability or (2) also did something to persuade him that Smoothflesh was preferable to Freshface. But where is such a criterion to be found? The only objective datum is the individual's preference; it is the observable fact that Mr. A formerly brought Freshface and now buys Smoothflesh after reading the advertisements. Those are the facts.

Value of advertising from the advertiser's point of view

Such facts as these and not *a priori* reasoning should be our starting point. The suitability of this common-sense approach is indicated by examining the reasons for advertising. No one pays to advertise his products in order to establish the eternal verities. All advertising is persuasive in intent. Since we cannot identify the distinction between informative and

[1] *Economist* (November 23, 1946), 822f.

persuasive advertising by reference to the experience of either of the two persons affected, either the consumer reading the advertisement or the advertiser himself, it seems better to leave the distinction to the realm of ideas where it properly belongs.

Are we then to give up the search for a criterion of usefulness in advertising and give up the right to an opinion as to what advertising is wasteful and what is not?

At this stage again, sense is of more assistance than *a priori* reasoning. There is a general feeling among the public that it is spending too much on advertising. It is unlikely that this feeling is entirely meaningless and, upon investigation, we find that it is not.

Let us approach the question from the angle of the advertiser and ask the question why the seller, whether manufacturer or wholesale or retail trader, decides to spend money on advertisement? Although we said that two per cent of the *national* income was spent on advertisement this is a book-keeping concept and what happens is that the manufacturer or trader spends money on advertisement and recoups himself (i.e. covers the cost of advertisement) by increasing the selling price of the advertised (or other) product.

The seller advertises because he thinks that advertisement is the *cheapest* of various effective means of appealing to consumer interest and thereby of selling his goods. Since the seller has every incentive to make no mistake in this matter, serious grounds must be forthcoming to establish a case that he is mistaken in what is very much his business.

Advertising and the principle of substitution

It seems likely that in respect of *his* business, he is not mistaken. His problem is comparable to that of the manufacturer who can use a number of techniques in the production of a given article: "At the beginning of his undertaking, and at every successive stage, the alert business man strives so to modify his arrangements as to obtain better results with a given expenditure, or equal results with a less expenditure. In other words, he ceaselessly applies the principle of substitution, with the purpose of increasing his profits; and, in doing so, he seldom fails to increase the total efficiency of work, the total power over nature which man derives from organization and knowledge."[1] The principle of substitution is equally effectively at work when the seller decides to spend money on advertisement instead of on alternative means of selling his goods. This last is the point requiring emphasis: advertisement costs are, in origin, a substitute for costs of labour and transport which the manufacturer would incur if he employed alternative means of marketing his goods. Pushing this point a little further: the manufacturer might decide to spread information about the availability of his product, not by advertisement, but by sending out travellers with samples to visit wholesalers and/or retailers and explain to them by word of mouth what it was that he had to sell. Or again, he might rely entirely on the wholesaler to market his produce; the wholesaler would then employ the travellers. The manufacturer, in either of these circumstances, would be saved the cost of advertising; he would instead incur the cost of employing travellers or wholesalers to do the work.

When some such figure as £89 million is given as the annual expenditure on advertising for the nation as a whole it should be emphasized that, from the point of view of social accounting, the economies in transport and labour costs resulting from this action should simultaneously be instanced. The advertiser chooses what in his view is the cheapest and most effective means of enlisting consumer interest in his product. There is a further point: advertising provides a substantial proportion of the revenue of the Press. The consumer would have to pay more for newspapers and magazines were it not for advertising. Borden[2] estimates that in the United States one-fifth of total advertising outlay is returned to the consumer in this way. Should the consumer leave it at that, delegating decision in this matter, as it were, to the expert? It still remains to answer the question: is the total expenditure on advertising, which in fact

[1]Marshall, *Principles of Economics*[3] (1920), 355.

[2]Borden, *Economic Effects of Advertising*, U.S. (1944), 52: "With relatively few exceptions, advertising is an essential source of revenue to the 13,000 magazines and newspapers of the country. It has supplied some 60 per cent. to 70 per cent of the revenue of these publications. . . . Advertising practically alone supports radio broadcasting in the United States. p. 71; "thus, almost half the total advertising expenditure of some $824,000,000 in these media (newspapers, magazines and radio) was, in effect, returned to consumers in the form of low-cost periodicals and free radio entertainment."

eventuates, the right amount from the consumer's point of view?

Where market conditions are *imperfectly competitive*, as they inherently are in the field of trade, there is no reason to suppose that the operation of the principle of substitution will result in that solution of the economic problem which is most economic from the consumers' point of view.

Can wasteful advertising be defined?

If the extent of advertising is closely related to the type of market in which the advertised goods are sold, then we should be able to find *institutional* evidence of market conditions which are likely to produce more or less advertising and, finally, criteria by which to estimate excessive advertising.

The institutional criterion

These ideas will become more definite as we proceed to examinine the facts. The general thesis is that waste is not something inherent in particular types of advertising but that excessive advertising (defined as advertising which absorbs a larger proportion of scarce resources: land, labour and capital—than the community would voluntarily choose) will be recognized by an examination of the market conditions in which particular advertising originated.

The first step is, then, to find out by whom, in what manner and at which periods advertising is undertaken.

American data

Apart from the greater use of the radio in the U.S. and the fact that advertising absorbs an even greater proportion of the national income in the United States than in this country, (some 3 per cent instead of 2.2 per cent of the national income in 1935), the economics of advertising are substantially similar in the two countries.

Manufacturers are the largest advertisers of their products; advertising by large-scale retailers comes next and wholesalers, in the aggregate, advertise very little.

United States official data[1] show that in 1940 the average

[1]Federal Trade Commission on Distribution Methods and Costs, Part V. *Advertising as a Factor in Distribution*, U.S. (1944).

expenditure per dollar of sales by manufacturers[1] was 1.87 cents. The comparable percentage at the retail[2] level was 1.42 per cent, while advertising at the wholesale level[3] was negligible: .35 per cent or .35 of one cent per dollar of sales. No comparable data are available for this country but it seems clear that here, too, manufacturers are the largest advertisers and wholesalers have to the least extent substituted advertising for alternative sales techniques.

The position is readily understandable. The manufacturer or processor advertises his goods in order to introduce new products to maintain and extend consumer interest in established brands or products and to shift demand from competing products in the direction of his own. Advertising provides the manufacturer with a means of direct contact with the final consumer and by this means a measure of independence of the trader. The increasing use of advertisements is usually related to the progressive tendency of large-scale manufacturers to brand their goods and to by-pass the wholesaler. It is tempting to over-simplify this relationship. Both tendencies may themselves result from more fundamental causes—namely, the imperfections of the market. Lever[4] argues that "without the

[1]id. VIII, 2,549 manufacturing corporations with total sales $25,864,135,000 (1940) in different industry groups were investigated and they were found to have spent $483,503,000 on advertising in that year.

[2]id. X, 1,527 retailers with aggregate net sales (1939), $481,156,224 were examined and they were found to have spent $6,823,402 for advertising in that year.

[3]id. X, 439 wholesalers with aggregate net sales $439,215,815 were examined and they were found to have spent (1939) $1,552,094 on advertising.

[4]cf. Lever, *Advertising and Economic Theory* (1947), 30 "In the early days of mass production of consumption goods—during the nineteenth century this—buyers and sellers were usually brought together by wholesalers, who also tended to specify the goods to be made. Manufacturers, however, found that "wholesaler-dominated" markets and "shopping" goods were not wholly satisfactory to them. A particular disadvantage was that they tended to find their scope for expansion (e.g. to achieve the economies of larger scale production), limited by many wholesalers' traditional ways of doing business. Where markets were too restricted to permit of large-scale manufacture, the producers necessarily remained small. Consequently many firms began to seek to expand, and to assure markets for their production, by creating their own goodwill with the consuming public by supplying more and more convenience goods which were readily identifiable as being of their manufacture. Hence the modern use of trade-marks. Consumers were made "trade-mark conscious" by advertising, and anonymous, unidentifiable products became of less importance. Without the use of advertising the effects of manufacturers to free themselves from dependence on wholesalers would probably not have succeeded."

use of Advertising the efforts of manufacturers to free themselves from dependence on wholesalers would probably not have succeeded." But why were the manufacturers so anxious to free themselves from dependence on wholesalers? Lever refers to the wholesalers' "traditional ways of doing business" as standing in the manufacturers' way. This is the clue. Because of the imperfections of the market combined with an unstable level of industrial activity (see Chapter V) wholesalers ceased to perform their true economic functions efficiently. The free play of market forces as described in competitive theory was thus circumscribed by practices like resale price maintenance and was in any case impeded by the inherent imperfections of wholesale and retail trading; factors like geographical separation of buyers from other buyers and from sellers and lack of knowledge.

The feeling that this is so no doubt underlies the attempt to define the legitimacy of advertising in terms of its assistance in removing one source of market imperfection, namely, lack of knowledge, by spreading information concerning the availability of supplies. It falls down on the impossibility of distinguishing informative from persuasive advertising. The new approach suggested here is that advertising should be considered as an instrument for achieving control of the market. Some of the monopolist's aims are identical with those of the consuming public, for instance, both would prefer, other things being equal, that a given article should be produced as cheaply as possible. The use of machinery enables a larger output to be produced at reduced cost per unit: manufacturers may be prevented from achieving the maximum economies of large-scale production by inability to market larger outputs. It is in the interests of the community in such cases that the manufacturer should extend his market by advertising.[1] To look at advertising from this angle does not therefore in the least imply that all advertising is harmful. Some monopolistic practices may be harmful and some may be good; the criterion of their legitimacy, from the consumer's point of view is whether or

[1]Borden, *Economic Effects of Advertising* (1942) 489, Part 3, ch. xix, has collected valuable case history on the effects of advertising on production costs in the United States. There is little information of this kind in Britain.

not they are "in restraint of trade", that is, tending to prevent the most economic allocation of resources. The criterion applies to both public and private enterprise.

Manufacturers aim to create and maintain consumer preference by advertising

To illustrate this point: when the manufacturer advertises his product he achieves, if he is successful, a certain degree of preference for his commodity in the mind of the consumer resulting in increased sales. Manufacturers usually combine advertising directed to the final consumer with advertising directed to the retailer and possibly also to the wholesaler. Whether or not this is done, the manufacturer *automatically* as a result of affecting the final consumer's preference affects the trader's preference for the advertised article in so far as the consumers, *his* customers, will come in and ask for this product. Their estimate of his efficiency as a shopkeeper will be affected by whether or not he has in stock what they, the customers, want. Manufacturers' advertising restricts, in this sense, the trader's complete freedom of choice in the matter of what goods he shall make available. The shopper by this means also increases *his* bargaining power: he appears now not in the guise of a searcher after truth about availabilities from the lips of the shopkeeper but as asking to be supplied with a specific product. While it was observed in Chapter III that the shopper was tending more and more to hand over to the distributive trades the burden of choice, the availability of advertised brands provides the lazy consumer with a painless way of maintaining, nevertheless, his ascendency over the shopkeeper![1] Once the consumer has made his choice, there is, from his point of view, a very real gain in the availability of advertised brands; he at least knows how he can repeat a successful experiment.

[1] Bishop, *The Economics of Advertising* (1944), 29f, quotes the *Encyclopaedia Britannica,* 11th edition, article on "Advertising" as follows and refers to the buyer's "vague sense of antagonism towards the seller. There is a rudimentary feeling that even the most ordinary transaction of purchase brings into contact two minds actuated by diametrically opposed interests. . . . If he (the purchaser) has seen any one soap so persistently advertised that his memory retains its name, he will ask for it, not because he has any reason to believe it to be better or cheaper than others, but simply because he baffles the shopkeeper and assumes an authoritative attitude by exerting his own freedom of choice."

Relationship between advertising and resale price maintenance

Manufacturers often argue that the advertisement of a branded article *at a standard price* is required to achieve the full efficiency of advertising both from the manufacturers' and the consumers' point of view. It is a fact that "branded goods which are widely advertised . . . are nearly always price maintained."[1] It is argued in Chapter VIII that, whether or not this is so, the disadvantages of resale price maintenance of this kind, at any rate at the retail level, outweigh this benefit the consumer derives from knowing, over a considerable period of time, the exact price he will have to pay for a known brand.

The manufacturers have another argument in favour of resale price maintenance at the retail level as a necessary adjunct of successful advertising: it is that traders will, unless restrained by some external sanction, have a strong inducement themselves to advertise a product which is nationally advertised by its manufacturer at "cut prices", thus obtaining an allegedly unfair advantage over competitive traders and dissipating the effects of the manufacturer's advertising. The manufacturer fears that the consumer will argue as follows. If one trader can sell Smoothflesh Soapless Shaving Soap for 1/8, then others who are selling an identical article for 1/10 must be profiteering. This discredits the article in the consumers' eyes. The manufacturers have a further point: they argue that the very activity of thought, occasioned by this supposed debate in the consumer's mind, tends to dissipate the effect of his advertising. Watkins[2] argues that the success of advertising depends on the subordination of salesmanship: bargaining must be as far as possible eliminated. He refers to the "destructive shafts of counter-suggestion attendant on the consumer's evaluation of relative prices which takes place in price competition."

These arguments are convincing. Price competition lessens the efficiency of advertising and resale price maintenance increases the impact of a given advertisement on the consumer. But it cannot therefore be argued that advertisers have *ipso facto*

[1]Board of Trade: *Restraint of Trade*; *Report of Committee appointed by the Lord Chancellor and the President of the Board of Trade to consider certain Trade Practices* (1931).

[2]Watkins, *Public Regulation of Competitive Practices in Business Enterprise*, U.S. (1940).

the right to maintain the resale prices of their goods. Price competition is, just as much as advertising, a means of soliciting custom and the right of traders to choose between these business methods should not arbitrarily be circumscribed. There is some force, however, in the argument that the retailer who uses a given advertised brand as a price leader is wrongfully appropriating some of the manufacturer's expenditure to his own uses, but if the resale price of the advertised commodity is maintained, the trader's inducement to use it as a fighting line to advertise his own shop is to that extent increased. If the use of fighting lines by the shopkeeper or wholesaler to advertise *his* business is considered to be equivalent to a misappropriation of the manufacturer's advertising expenditure, it should then be proscribed as an unfair business practice.

Wholesalers' and retailers' aim in advertising

The question of traders' interest in advertising arises at this point. The proportion of advertising expenditure to total sales is highest at the manufacturing level and higher at retail than at wholesale.

The trader's purpose is to advertise his services as trader rather than to make consumers prefer any particular commodity in his stock. There is thus an immediate divergence of interest between the manufacturer and the trader. This has already been observed in the case of resale price maintenance and the use of "price leaders" but it is also generally true. The trader advertises a given brand only as a means of advertising his store and he tends to emphasize price, style, quality, service and business integrity. Because his aim is to advertise his business, the trader tends to shift from one product to another in his advertising and to advertise those commodities which are currently most popular with the type of customer to whom *he* is appealing. This is unsatisfactory from the manufacturer's point of view. The creation of consumer preference by means of advertising is a long-term business; advertising to be successful must be continuous and prolonged. The manufacturer has therefore tried, by co-operative advertising[1], that is by making

[1]The term "co-operative advertising" has been used in a different sense to mean advertising the product of an entire industry, for example, the advertisement of Milk and Milk products by the Milk Marketing Board.

advertising by the distributor a condition of sale of his products, to secure more continuous advertisement of his products by traders who deal in them.

Co-operative advertising in the United States

Co-operative advertising has been adopted in the United States. Arrangements vary[1]: sometimes manufacturers and distributors both contribute to a joint fund for local advertising supervised by the manufacturer; or, alternatively, an allowance is made by the manufacturer to some or all dealers to cover a portion of dealers' advertising of the manufacturer's product; or, finally, an allowance of trade-marked materials to the buyer may be made by the manufacturer as in the case of textiles. The principle is the same in all: manufacturers secure the co-operation of traders in the continuous advertisement of their product and insure themselves against the trader's natural tendency to shift from advertising one product to another.

This development is extremely interesting from our general standpoint that the important factor in determining whether or not advertising costs are excessively burdensome to the trade is closely related to the degree of competition in the market for the advertised product. We shall return to this point at the end of the Chapter. Let us first see how the extent of advertising is related not to types of market but to types of commodity and also how far the level of expenditure on advertising is related to the state of trade.

Where is advertising expenditure greatest?

Reference has just been made to the traders' practice of making frequent variations in the product advertised with the overriding purpose of advertising their business. The result of this is that it is exceedingly difficult to compute the total expenditure on advertising, at all trading levels, for particular commodity groups. Several[2] attempts have been made, however, to estimate manufacturers' expenditure on advertising

[1]Report of the Federal Trade Commission on *Distributive Methods and Costs,* U.S. (1944), Part V, Advertising as a Factor in Distribution, viii ff.

[2]cf. Federal Trade Commission, *Distribution Methods and Costs,* (1944) Part V, 7 ff.

particular commodity groups and these estimates confirm the following general conclusions:[1]

(1) The amount expended on advertising by manufacturers varies enormously between industries.

(2) Within certain industries, notably food, the advertising practice of manufacturers varies widely.

(3) Advertising is mainly directed to consumers' goods in contrast to, for example, semi-finished goods or heavy chemicals.

United States data

The advertising of 2,716 manufacturing corporations in ninety-one industry groups investigated by the United States Federal Trade Commission[2] ranged from a minimum of six hundredths of one cent per dollar of sales in the shipbuilding industry to a maximum of 13.94 cents in drugs and medicines. Of the 41 industries showing the lowest proportion of advertising costs to net sales,[3] all with advertising expenditure less than 1 per cent of net sales, none manufactured to an important extent for the final consumer. The heavily advertised products (for this purpose defined as those industries where the average expenditure on advertising is more than 3 per cent of net sales) are, in contrast, all consumer's goods. They are (the figures in brackets show the average advertising costs as a percentage of net sales): Drugs and medicines (13.94); cereal preparations

[1] *Economist* (Nov. 23, 1946) "The Costs of Advertising," Reports on the figures contained in the forthcoming report of the National Institute of Economic and Social Research, *Statistics of Advertising*.

[2] Federal Trade Commission Report on *Distribution Methods and Costs*, U.S. (1944), 5ff.

[3] Federal Trade Commission, id. 6: Listed in ascending order of magnitude of advertising expenditure as a percentage of net sales they are: shipbuilding, crude petroleum, merchant pig iron, copper smelting and refining, cane sugar refining, beet sugar manufacturing, bolts, etc., lumber and timber products, textile dyeing and finishing, steel castings, tanned leather, aircraft manufacture, iron and steel forgings, lead and zinc products, match manufacturing, grey and malleable iron castings, woollen and worsted manufacturing, clay products (except pottery) railroad equipment, electric wire and cable, screw machine products, lead and zinc primary smelting, coke oven products, power boilers, etc., cotton textiles, machine tool accessories, oil-feed machinery, tin cans and tinware, machine tools, steam engines and turbines, plastics manufacturing, paper and paper pulp, fertilizer manufacturing, mining machinery and equipment, cement, rayon and allied products, industrial chemicals, plumbers' supplies, automobile accessories and parts, textile machinery, special industry machines.

(13.08); cigarettes (11.30); soaps and cooking fats (10.94); distilled liquors (9.79); malt beverages (8.97); tobacco products (8.20), cigars (5.40), fruit and vegetable canning (4.49), men's and boys' clothing (4.20).

Wholesalers' advertising totalling $1,552,094 (1939) in relation to total net sales of $439,215,815, an average expenditure of 35 one hundredths of one cent per dollar of net sales, ranged from a minimum of 3 one hundredths of one cent for men's and boys' clothing to a maximum of 1.08 cents for paint and varnish.

Retailers' advertising totalling $6,823,402 (1939) in relation to total net sales of $481,156,224, an average of 1.42 cents per sales dollar, ranged from a minimum of 59 one hundredth of a cent, for lumber to a maximum of 4.33 cents for women's clothing.

Basing his estimate on display advertising in the press, only one of the available media, Bishop[1] lists the percentage of total expenditure on advertising in Britain by leading commodity groups and services as follows: Food and drink, 18.3 per cent; household supplies, 12.9 per cent; Medicines, 11.0 per cent; Wearing Apparel, 10.9 per cent; Transport, 10.0 per cent; Toilet, 9.8 per cent; Financial, 6.5 per cent; Entertainment, 6.3 per cent; smoking, 6.1 per cent; and miscellaneous, 8.2 per cent.

He relates this expenditure, amounting in all to £28,619,552 for 1938, to consumer expenditure on the listed products of £2,550,000,000 for the same year[2] and finds the following results:

TABLE VI

United Kingdom: Estimated Advertising Expenditure as a Percentage of Total Retail Sales in 1938

Commodity Group	*Advertising Percentage*
Food	.86
Beer	.88
Wines and Spirits	2·80
Tobacco and Cigarettes	2·79
Clothing	1·88
Household Supplies	3·89
Books, Newspapers, Periodicals	2·40
Drugs, etc.	34·00

Source: Bishop, *Economics of Advertising*, 1949, pp. 100 and 101.

[1]Bishop, *Economics of Advertising* (1944), 38 Table [2]Bishop, id. 100f.

The total expenditure on advertising amounted to 2.30 per cent of total expenditure on these commodity groups. These figures are useful only in indicating (*a*) the commodity groups which are most heavily advertised in the Press (Press advertising is by far the most important medium in Britain) and (*b*) the relative expenditures on Press advertising for these groups. No direct comparison with the United States data is feasible because no data on the proportion of Press advertising conducted at the manufacturers' level is available nor is there information on the other advertising media.

These averages conceal the important fact that the level of advertising costs varies widely *within* a given industry. Taking food as an example: In the United Kingdom two-fifths of advertising expenditure on food relates to goods carrying an advertising charge of less than 3 per cent whereas the average advertising charge for the remaining three-fifth of expenditure is 12.2 per cent.[1] The same result holds for the United States.

TABLE VII

United States: Importance of Advertising as a factor in the distribution expense of manufacturers per dollar of net sales of foods, 1939[2]

Food	Advertising and Sales Promotion Percentage of net sales	Total Distribution Expense percentage of net sales	Percentage of advertising to total distribution costs
Cereals	8.01	30.85	25·98
Coffee	5·26	20·66	25·44
Biscuits	4·74	29·72	15·96
Flour	4·54	13·17	34·49
Canned fruits	1·97	10·64	18·54
Meats	·46	5·57	8·32
Sugar	·20	3·87	5·28

Source: U.S. Federal Trade Commission

The above figures show not only the wide variation in advertising costs within a given commodity group but they

[1]*Economist* (Nov. 23, 1946), quoted from the then unpublished report of the National Institute of Economic and Social Research.

[2]Compiled from Report of Federal Trade Commission, Report on *Distribution Methods and Costs* (1944-8) Table 2.

show also that where advertising costs are heavy, they tend to be a larger proportion of total distribution costs. There are, however, important exceptions to this general rule. The combination of high advertising costs with low selling costs is typical of drugs, patent medicines and cereal preparations. Low advertising costs and high selling costs characterize those manufactures which require servicing during their lifetime like sewing machines, office equipment: or the marketing of which is for other reasons costly like bakery products. On the other hand, the combination of low advertising costs and low selling costs is typical of the makers of heavy capital goods, raw or partly finished manufactured products and a few consumers' goods like sugar-products.

If then we regard the correlation between high advertising and high distribution costs as sufficiently representative to constitute a general rule, we have to consider it in relation to the possibility of substituting advertising for other methods of selling. Does the above general rule[1] imply simply that to advertise a commodity at all effectively is an expensive business? Borden holds that advertising is not homogeneous, isolated or unique. It is an integral part of a business plan. Or does it imply that there is something in the character of advertising expenditure which makes it cumulative? Investigation has not been carried sufficiently far to give a definitive answer to these questions, but that there is a serious possibility that advertising expenditures are cumulative is implied throughout the present discussion.

Advertising is a symptom of monopoly

Advertising is a symptom of monopoly. There would be no advertising in a competitive market. The competitive market supposes that all buyers and sellers are similarly placed with respect to the sale of a homogeneous commodity. In such a market where both buyers and sellers are numerous, the

[1]Federal Trade Commission, id. 9. "Those commodities in all groups respecting which manufacturers carry the identification of their products to the consumer generally have both the largest total distribution expense and the largest advertising expense per dollar of sales. Advertising expended on such commodities generally represents relatively large proportions of their total distribution expense."

individual seller has no occasion to advertise in order to extend his market since he can market all he can produce without incurring sales resistance. Advertising necessarily relates to a non-homogeneous product. "The commodities in all three groups that bear the largest advertising per dollar of sales are those for which manufacturers' brands are promoted most extensively as a means of identifying and differentiating the products to the consumer."[1] Like all monopolistic practices, advertising by one seller tends to induce competitive (or defensive) advertising on the part of others. Reference was made above to the practice of "co-operative" advertising in the United States. This is an excellent example of institutional arrangements which lead to excessive advertising. The best means of identifying advertising as excessive from the community's point of view, that is to say, the best pointer to excess, is the market conditions which generated the advertising. What better evidence of excess could be adduced than the advertisers' own opinion that the cost of advertising is mounting in spite of their individual wish and to little purpose? "The fact that manufacturer A offers dealers a co-operative advertising deal soon causes dealers of manufacturers B, C and D to demand a similar deal. Failure by B, C and D to offer similar dealer co-operation produces dealer dissatisfaction. But as soon as co-operative advertising becomes the practice of all competing manufacturers, some, at least, of its benefits are lost to the companies first using it, and the industry may find itself saddled with a distribution expense which may or may not be productive of volume warranting the expenditure."[2] Many witnesses before the Federal Trade Commission characterized the insistent demands of retail traders for co-operative advertising allowances as "a highly undesirable trade practice."[3]

[1]Federal Trade Commission, id., 9.

[2]Federal Trade Commission, id., XIV.

[3]Federal Trade Commission, id. XIII: The case of the American manufacturers of rayon. The case for co-operative advertising of rayon is strong because it must be done by advertising products fabricated from rayon yarn. Yet, the cost of co-operative advertising had become so burdensome that, in 1939, at a conference of rayon producers and a committee of weavers, the principal rayon producers, except one, agreed to discontinue haring any of the cost of advertising with retail distributors, cutters, con-sert ers or weavers."

Others considered it unfair and discriminatory in so far as some traders may be excluded and others may simply pocket the manufacturers' allowance. Since detailed supervision of the trader's advertising by the manufacturer would be costly, co-operative advertisers lay themselves open to the charge of discrimination where the advertising allowances have not been afforded to all traders "proportionately on equal terms" as required by the Robinson-Patman Act.

Can advertising expenditures be regulated in the public interest?

Where there is reason to suppose that the burden of advertising is increasing under the stimulus of imperfect competition—and the evidence of the manufacturers concerned will be the best guide—there will be a case for state intervention to restrain the extension of advertising in that field.

The community is interested not only in the total cost of advertising but also in the efficiency of advertising—that is, in whether this money is well spent. With the above qualification, we should recommend that the advertiser himself is the best person to take this decision and that qualification is that he must have information on consumer preferences and the availability of substitutes in order to take an informed decision. The manufacturer, wholesaler or retailer who is paying to advertise[1] wants his advertising to be successful. It is unlikely that he can afford extensive preliminary market research; even if he could, for each manufacturer to conduct his own market research is a needless duplication and a wasteful use of capital and labour. Market research should be conducted on an industry basis financed by a compulsory levy on all firms within the industry and made available to all members.[2]

[1]Most advertisement is conducted by advertising agencies, on behalf of manufacturers, wholesalers and retailers. cf. Bishop, *The Economics of Advertising*, 66ff.

[2]cf. Recommendations made by the Board of Trade Working Parties. For example the following:

Hosiery (1946) 30. "The first need is for the provision of a full range of statistics easily accessible to all firms."

Lace (1947), III "We are of the opinion that there is a strong case for the compulsory finance of economic and market research on the grounds that . . . all firms in the industry stand to gain. . . ."

Heavy clothing (1947), 35: "The present arrangements for the collection and dissemination of information of interest to clothing manufacturers are

Borden considers that the following factors are favourable to the successful use of advertising:

A. The trend of demand in the particular industry should be rising. It is unlikely that advertising will do more than delay the impact of generally decreasing demand or hasten the arrival of generally increasing demand though it can, of course, affect the share of total demand accruing to a particular firm.

B. There should be an opportunity to stimulate selective demand, i.e. brand preference for a particular product. This opportunity is most likely to be present under such circumstances as the following:

1. When there is substantial chance for differentiation of product.

2. When consumer satisfaction depends largely on hidden qualities that cannot easily be judged at the time of purchase for instance, toilet soap as contrasted with green vegetables.

3. When strong emotional buying motives exist, such as protection of health or enhancement of social position.

C. The combination of potential unit sales multiplied by the rate of gross margin must be high enough to permit necessary advertising expenditure in the particular market.

It is clear that the advertiser has little hope of taking a reasoned decision in these matters without extensive market research. It is to the interest of consumer and advertisers alike that money and resources devoted to advertising should not be wasted. Item C, however, points once more to the criterion of excessive advertising by reference to the inducement which monopoly profits might provide to an exaggerated advertising effort.

Otherwise, there is a strong case for regarding the progressive substitution of advertising for alternative techniques of salesmanship as the result of its admitted usefulness.

---

inadequate and unsatisfactory . . . Many of the medium and small firms, the great majority of whom could profit from such information, are not normally in a position to incur the expense of obtaining it for themselves." The Working Party therefore recommends the creation of a Central Information Bureau for the industry.

Jewellery and Silverware (1946), 36: "We recommend that the industry as a whole should plan for itself and set up a central organisation under its own control, to carry out consumer research. . . ."

CHAPTER VIII

RESALE PRICE MAINTENANCE AND TRADE ASSOCIATION

Presumption that resale price maintenance is uneconomic or wasteful

It was stated in Chapter III that a number of goods had to be sold at fixed prices set by manufacturers and that where resale price maintenance of this kind was practised, price competition as envisaged by much economic analysis could not occur at all. In Chapter IV, it was argued that the practice of resale price maintenance led to (*a*) a variety of forms of non-price competition; (*b*) a greater number of small-scale independent retail shops than there would otherwise be and (*c*) discrimination against the newer types of large-scale retailer whose main competitive weapon was the price appeal. The purpose of the present chapter is to apply this analysis to the facts.

There is a very strong presumption on theoretical grounds that the practice of resale price maintenance (the practice by which minimum wholesale and retail prices or margins for the resale of goods are fixed by producers) prevents the movement of the greatest quantity of goods at the lowest prices, hinders the economic distribution of resources and, thereby, prevents the maximization of living standards.

Where monopoly is present there is no necessary coincidence between private and public interest

It will be assumed, in what follows, that there is general agreement that wherever an element of monopoly is present, the individual trader's or manufacturer's pursuit of gain does not necessarily result in the most economic allocation of resources from the community's point of view. Neither, of course, is monopolistic action *ipso facto* uneconomic from the community's standpoint. An element of monopoly is defined as the power of the individual seller to control the price at which he markets his output.[1] Trade Association action to effect resale price maintenance is an example of the exercise of such a power.

[1]This proposition rests on the following argument: Once the producer is in a position to influence market prices (which involves the assumption of diminishing demand price for increased output), it pays him to sell a smaller output at a higher price than would prevail in competitive conditions. In figure V DD[1] is the demand curve showing the maximum price consumers will pay for outputs (shown along OX) mr is the marginal revenue curve, mc is the marginal cost curve, ac is the average (total) cost curve.

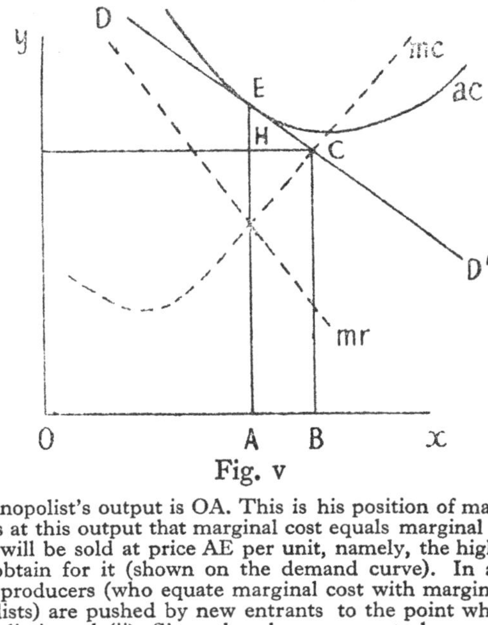

Fig. v

The monopolist's output is OA. This is his position of maximum profit because it is at this output that marginal cost equals marginal revenue. The output OA will be sold at price AE per unit, namely, the highest price the seller can obtain for it (shown on the demand curve). In a competitive market, (i) producers (who equate marginal cost with marginal revenue as do monopolists) are pushed by new entrants to the point where abnormal profits are eliminated (ii) Since they have no control over market price, marginal revenue for them is identical with demand price (v., Figure I, p. 33). The competitive producer's interest is, thus, to increase output up to the point where marginal cost equals *price*, ac is the average (total) cost curve. Total, in this context, refers to the inclusion of both prime (variable) and overhead (fixed) costs. In diagram the output which would prevail in competition (where all producers equate marginal cost with price) is OB and this output will be marketed for the highest price it will fetch BC.

Under monopoly then the price will be higher (by EH) and the output lower (by AB) than under competition.

We have thus shown that the monopolist's interest is not necessarily equivalent to that of the community.

Large-scale production makes free competition and the uncontrolled operation of the pricing system less likely

It was inevitable, once big business came into play alongside little business, that managerial discretion should compromise and supersede the higgling of the market. Because the economies of large-scale operation are far greater in the field of industry than in the field of trade, the anti-social character of monopolistic activity was first demonstrated at the production level and received much public recognition. The economies of scale are not so widely or universally available in the field of distributive trade as they are in the field of production, particularly of manufacture. Decentralized distribution is the corollary of centralized production. Yet, at the present time, both in this country and the United States, the substitution of managerial discretion for the uncontrolled operation of the pricing system is no less widespread in the field of distributive trading than in the field of production. The main differences are that it is effected by agreement among small businesses, that it is not necessarily or even normally attended by any compensating economies of large-scale operation and that it takes place without public or general recognition of the fact.

Trade Associations and the control of competition

Such a wide variety of techniques is used and the principal organizations practising them—the Trade Associations—have remained so carefully in the background of publicity[1] that the facts of the case, in so far as this country is concerned, are little understood.[2] In the United States, among many other sources, the voluminous and illuminating reports of the Temporary National Economic Committee, written at the beginning of the war, provide ample illustrative material and a realistic

[1]Levy, *Retail Trade Associations*, (1942) ("What is notable among British consolidations and associations is not their variety or weakness so much as their unobtrusiveness. There is not much display in the window, but there is a good selection inside.")

[2]The issues involved are, however, very numerous and, in some respects, as for instance where reductions in cost of production which will both increase the monopolist's profits and lead to reduced prices, the interests of the monopolist coincide with those of the community. The reader is referred to *Monopoly*, E. A. G. Robinson, Cambridge University Press, 1941, for a discussion of the issues involved.

analysis of the problems. The problem at present confronting both countries is to find some formula for reconciling the pursuit of gain with the prohibition against monopoly, for it is equally true of both countries that "once it is realized that business monopoly paralyses the system of free enterprise on which it is grafted, and is as fatal to those who manipulate it as to the people who suffer beneath its impositions, action by the Government to eliminate these artificial restraints will be welcomed by industry throughout the nation."[1]

The economic issues involved in both countries are substantially similar and American experience in connection with attempts to control business practices and in particular resale price maintenance, throws a powerful light on many of our own problems. The legal background in the two countries is, however, dissimilar. A brief review of American attempts to control business practices by legislation reveals the more important forces at work, particularly the intricacies of trying to maintain competition in what is the inherently imperfectly competitive field of distribution.

The combination of protection from foreign competition and the absence of legal restraint of monopolistic practices which has prevailed in Britain for the last decade and a half has encouraged the adoption of monopolistic practices.

Such is not the case in the United States, where public recognition of the uneconomic character of many monopolistic practices was translated into legal prohibition at an early date.[2] The passage of the Sherman Anti-Trust Act, in 1890, made illegal every combination in restraint of trade.

Sherman Act, 1890

The Sherman Act was intended to bring about an improvement in business ethics which had deteriorated during the period of bad trade following the American Civil War. Recurrent spasms of cut-throat competition indicated the general

[1]Temporary National Economic Committee on the Concentration of Economic Power, appointed by Executive Order, 1938. Monograph No. 18, *Trade Association Survey*.

[2]An excellent discussion of legal restraint on monopoly in the United States is contained in Watkins, *Public Regulation of Competitive Practices in Business Enterprise*, New York (1940).

deterioration. Though it contained no specific prohibition of unfair practices, it was interpreted in the Courts as providing for the regulation of competitive tactics, but only where a firm or business had acquired a dominating position in a given industry. There was thus no method of reaching unfair competitive practices where they were conducted by small business enterprises. Prosperity, after 1900, had a salutary effect on the level of business ethics and industrial leaders pressed insistently for either a legislative or administrative definition of exact standards of competitive conduct. It was in the interests of the "good" monopolists to prevent the uneconomic business practices of small men: the assumption underlying the Sherman Act had seemed to be that only big businesses were likely to use illegitimate business tactics. The general desire was for competition but for competition free from unfair or deceptive practices.

Clayton Act and Federal Trade Commission Act, 1914

The passage of the Clayton Act and the Federal Trade Commission Act in 1914 was intended to fulfil these desires on the basis of *non-discrimination.* The Clayton Act declared illegal any discrimination in price (except discrimination based on differences in quality or in quantity) as between different purchasers, where the effect might be substantially to lessen competition. At the same time the Federal Trade Commission was set up to administer the proscription of unfair methods of competition.

Agitation for legal recognition of resale price maintenance

The economic forces of the inter-war period making for the limitation of price competition were, however, so strong that agitation arose after the First World War for the amendment of the Sherman Act in the direction of a more severe restriction of price discrimination, The agitation came primarily from the small trader. Legislation, in 1936, and 1937, showed that what had begun as a movement to secure the virtues of competition had developed into a means of guaranteeing the interests of a certain type of trading unit. The remarkable success of the business methods of the chain stores (v. Chapter IV), based on price competition, had aroused the violent opposition of the independent retail merchants and of those wholesalers whose interests were adversely affected by the chain stores' practice of large-scale purchase direct from the producer. This was the period of growing political influence of the middle class and the small scale merchants. The controversy over resale price maintenance epitomized these issues. The practice of resale price maintenance had long been subject to federal regulation,[1] and condemned in certain circumstances, even before the Sherman Act. The passage of the Robinson-Patman Act (1936) (to amend section 2 of the Clayton Act) closed a period of more than thirty years' legal restraint of the practice of resale price maintenance. The 1936 Act restricted the right of the seller to charge different prices to different buyers (price discrimination) by (*a*) putting the onus of justifying quantity discounts, as non-restrictive, on the seller, (*b*) authorizing the Federal Trade Commission to set arbitrary limits on the extent of price discrimination even where the price differentials corresponded to cost differentials, and (*c*) requiring 'allowances' to be made available to all buyers "proportionately on equal terms." The next year, in 1937, the political victory of the regular traders was completed by the passage of the Miller-Tydings Act which legalized resale price maintenance in inter-State commerce. Simultaneously the passage of so-called "Fair Trade" laws by numerous State governments secured for manufacturers and processors working within the limits of one State in the Federation an equivalent right to fix the minimum price at which the retailer could sell his output. By 1940, Fair Trade Regulation had been passed in some forty States in the Union. In some states the regular traders had even secured legislation requiring retailers not to sell at less than a fixed percentage mark-up over their cost price. This legislation discriminated directly against the chain stores.

It should be noted that the Miller-Tydings Act legalizing resale price maintenance in inter-state commerce was passed over the protest, both of the President of the United States and of the Federal Trade Commission and that more recently, in 1941, the Temporary National Committee on the Concentration of Economic Power reported in favour of its repeal.

[1]Watkins, id., 50.

The result of legislation, post-1936, legalizing resale price maintenance has been to weaken the operation of the Sherman Anti-Trust Act in the field of distribution and to permit a progress towards the proscription of price-competition and the adoption of techniques of non-price competition which is very comparable to our own experience.

Growth of resale price maintenance in Great Britain

In this country, competition by means of price reductions has progressively given way to the soliciting of custom by other means designed to increase the customers' preference for a particular brand of article or for a particular distributor. Resale price-maintenance (defined above) is extensively conducted by Trade Associations embracing manufacturers and/or wholesalers and/or retailers in a given trade. Attention has been drawn by public committees of investigation to the fact that during two periods in the present century, war has fostered the growth of these organizations and strengthened them. But the first associations originated not in the twentieth but in the nineteenth century and they originated not in the convenience of government but with the commercial objective of withholding supplies of controlled products from those who sold below an agreed price. However, the effect of wartime price administration[1] on the basis of conventional margins for all buyers has in Britain showed signs of weakening the hold of Trade Associations on their members and there are instances of practices like the grant of loyalty discounts being discontinued.

The legal position of individual managements in their practice of price maintenance is restricted only by the common law prohibition against "restraint of trade", which is very generously interpreted indeed. Trade Associations can enjoy the protection of a whole series of Trade Union Acts from 1871 to 1927.[2]

The legal position in Great Britain

A Trade Association is then a Trade Union, as defined in the Trade Union Act, 1876, Section 16. The term "Trade

[1]See Chapter IX below.

[2]Johnson-Davies, *Control in Retail Industry* (1945), 19ff.

Union" means "any combination, whether temporary or permanent, for regulating the relations between workmen and masters, or between workmen and workmen, or between masters and masters, or for imposing restrictive conditions on the conduct of any trade or business, whether such combination would or would not . . . have been deemed to be an unlawful combination by reason of some one or more of its purposes being in restraint of trade." In so far as a trade association has for its principal objective the imposition of restrictive conditions on the conduct of trade it is a Trade Union within the meaning of this Act.

Certain important results follow. Trade Associations enjoy the protection of the whole series of Trade Union Acts from 1871 to 1927 and Section 2 and 3 of the 1871 Act read: "The purposes of any trade union shall not, by reason merely that they are in restraint of trade, be deemed to be unlawful, so as to render any member of such a trade union liable to prosecution . . . ;" and "the purposes of any trade union shall not by reason merely that they are in restraint of trade be unlawful so as to render void or voidable any agreement or trust."[1] An important legal disability[2] is, however, imposed on Trade Associations by Section 4 of the Act of 1871 which renders "an agreement between members of a trade union concerning the conditions on which any members shall or shall not sell their goods . . ." not directly enforceable in Courts of Law.

The Trade Associations can thus obtain immunity against actions for damages which might (if they were not deemed trade unions) have been brought against them for committing what would otherwise have been actionable wrongs in the exercise of price maintenance. Effective price maintenance, however, requires that sanctions should be applied against those who sell below the permitted price. Yet there is no contractual obligation enforceable in the ordinary courts on the seller to conform to the agreed price. Trade Associations have, therefore, devised their own sanctions: the so-called "Stop List", a very powerful sanction indeed, whereby supplies are withheld from sellers adjudged by the association to have

[1]Johnson-Davies, id., 22.
[2]Johnson-Davies, id., 25.

infringed the regulations for price-maintenance. Trade Union status permits the withholding of supplies to such traders except where, in the view of the ordinary courts of law, the association has been guilty of "restraint of trade".

The current law with respect to restraint of trade was settled in 1894 by a House of Lords' decision[1] which reads as follows:

"The public has an interest in every person's carrying on his trade freely; so has the individual. All interference with individual liberty of action in trading, and all restraints of trade themselves, if there is nothing more, are contrary to public policy, and, therefore, void. That is the general rule. But there are exceptions: restraints of trade and interference with individual liberty of action may be justified by the special circumstances of a particular case. It is sufficient justification, and, indeed, it is the only justification if the restriction is reasonable—reasonable, that is, in reference to interests of the parties concerned and reasonable in reference to the interests of the public, so framed and so guarded as to afford adequate protection to the party in whose favour it is imposed, while, at the same time, it is in no way injurious to the public." The courts have not, in fact, excluded the enforcement of price-maintenance by the "Stop List" as restraint of trade but it is not in the least clear that the practice of resale price maintenance is in the public interest.

Extent of Trade Association

"Trade Associations in this country now number over two thousand."[2] "The end of the last and the first decades of the new century saw a decisive change from competitive to associative organization in almost every trade in Britain. . . . There is no difficulty now in finding examples of trade associations. They cover the whole field of retail business activities."[3]

Following the findings of the Committee on Restraint of Trade (1931)[4] the tendency has been to attribute the formation

[1]Johnson-Davies, id., 36. [2]Johnson-Davies, id., 2.
[3]Levy, *Retail Trade Associations* (1942), 20.
[4]Board of Trade, Report of Committee appointed by the Lord Chancellor and the President of the Board of Trade to consider certain trade practices. H.M. Stationery Office, 1931, p. 11.

of trade associations in this country to the "difficulties encountered by individual manufacturers seeking to maintain re-sale prices." All manufacturers are concerned, it is argued, to prevent general price-cutting in times of bad trade and also the sale of their particular goods at "cut-price" rates.

Motives behind resale price maintenance

American literature tends to emphasize the degree to which traders, particularly independent retailers, have been more than ready accessories to price-maintenance and have, in some cases, brought pressure to bear on manufacturers to determine minimum resale prices and margins. To take one illustration: the Sales Manager of a drug manufacturer writing on the subject of the "Fair Trade" legislation (vide above) which modified the Anti-Trust legislation as far as distribution was concerned, wrote in *Printers' Ink*, August 26th, 1937[1]:

> If he has followed the history of the fair-trade movement he should know that the laws were forced through by independent retailers, that very few manufacturers have taken an active part in obtaining passage. He should know, also, that in the drug and cosmetic field many manufacturers are being compelled to operate under these laws against their wisdom and better judgment. Pressure is being brought to bear through the retailers' associations and their fair-trade committees.
>
> Manufacturers who do not file minimum prices are having their troubles with independent outlets in some states. Those manufacturers such as ourselves who have filed prices have had to set higher minimums than they desired in some instances. The Committees are not permitted, supposedly, by law to dictate what the minimum prices shall be but they are doing just that by refusing to approve contracts containing prices which do not give the retailer what they consider to be a fair profit margin. In most cases the committees are insisting on a mark-up of at least 20 per cent. and usually 33⅓ per cent.

The difficulties experienced in Britain of effecting trade association among retailers and the absence of prohibitive legislation (which united retailers in opposition in the United States)

[1]Temporary National Economic Committee, *Investigation of Concentration of Economic Power*, Senate Committee Print, 76th Congress, 3rd Session, 88.

probably account for the more passive role played by British retailers in bringing about resale price maintenance.

There is ample evidence to show that, in both countries, as things are at present, both manufacturers and traders are not putting up any resistance to the progressive elimination of price competition. There is no economic force tending to limit this progress and if the elimination of price-competition is adjudged to lead to an uneconomic allocation of resources, legislation will be required to reorientate competitive methods.

The phrase price-competition was used advisedly. Much of the written work on the inter-war period talks in terms of the decline in or control of competition. Writers have referred to the progressive concentration of management first as a result of large-scale production, and secondly as the result of trust and cartel arrangements in these terms. Such concentration of management has indeed led to a change in the broad trend of business strategy and to an indubitable tendency to substitute expenditure on advertising and other methods of sales promotion for price appeals. The forms of non-price competition are very numerous and various. Perhaps the best indication of their character and variety is the classification given in the T.N.E.C. Monograph No. 1, pp. 94-98 (Price Behaviour and Business Policy), where two hundred and twenty-nine distinct methods are listed and placed in fourteen different categories. We have investigated the reasons for this change in business strategy but first we should emphasize that what has happened is not so much the suppression of competition but a change in the technique of competition and a shift away from price-competition.

The diseconomies of price competition

There seem to be three main reasons why large-scale producers have turned away from price competition.

Price-wars

First: price reductions were found to be a double-edged competitive weapon. Once a management takes into account the possibility that price reductions (intended to increase sales) may bring about price reductions on the part of its competitors, its attractions of price competition are reduced, probably eliminated. A market in which managements take into consideration the effect of changes in their price policy on the price policy of others has been called an oligopolistic market. Conditions of oligopoly[1] are widespread in this country and in the United States. They are bound to result, sooner or later, from the concentration of economic power.

Progressive product differentiation reduces effectiveness of price competition

Secondly: industrialization leads to an increasing variety—differentiation—of products. A wide range of choice of consumer goods is one of the characteristics of a high standard of living. Yet price competition is most relevant to the sale of indistinguishable products. Only if the consumer is otherwise indifferent as between the products from two sources will a price differential determine his choice. Thus price reductions as a competitive weapon lose their efficacy once product differentiation becomes the rule.

Price stability is an aid to cost accounting

Thirdly: large-scale production requires a more or less complicated system of cost accounting. Management bases its decisions as to the most economical and the most efficient method of production for which it is (or should be) constantly searching, on price differentials on the side both of costs and of receipts. Fluctuating prices (either selling prices or the prices at which the managements buy their factors of production) make the process of computation much more difficult. Price-stability becomes a condition of accurate measurement.

[1]v. Hall and Hitch. *Oxford Economic Papers II.* "Price Theory and Business Behaviour." The trail blazed by Hall and Hitch has been pursued in the *Economic Journal* (September, 1947) by K. W. Rothschild in an article "Price Recovery and Oligopoly" (298ff.) Rothschild's conclusions include the following:

(1) "Price rigidity is an essential aspect of "normal" oligopolistic price strategy", 312.

(2) "Oligopolistic circumstances lead to a multitude of conditions surrounding the quoted price," 312.

(3) "Under oligopoly the price tends to be the outcome of a variety of conflicting tendencies within the firm, which have all to be taken into account if a full explanation is aimed at," 313.

Manufacturers fear that reductions in traders' margins may impair distributors' efficiency

Fourthly: as the manufacturers themselves frequently allege, they have an interest in the well-being of the commercial units which market their output. That the efficiency of the distributive trades is of major importance to the producer is well understood. That he sees resale price maintenance as a means of securing efficient retail distribution is less comprehensible. The attempt has been made in this book to explain how it is that the manufacturer in an imperfectly competitive market may consider such a practice to be in his interest while in reality it is only in his short term interest or even not in his interest at all in the sense that if his competitors were prevented from practising it, he would have no inducement to do so.

Will competitive forces, manufacturer versus trader, secure the narrowing of margins to cover costs?

There is a further point concerning the community's interest in this matter: it has been argued that a natural conflict of interest between manufacturers and distributors, residing in the manufacturers' desire to reduce prices wherever price reductions will lead to increased profits and to a consequent desire, other things being equal, for lower rather than higher distributors' margins, will prevent collusion between manufacturers and traders to cover excessive margins by unnecessary increases in final prices.

This tendency is in abeyance in conditions of inflation

It cannot be emphasized too strongly that this is not true in all circumstances. Whenever the combination of (*a*) a chronic scarcity of consumption goods and (*b*) the closely associated condition of inflation occurs, this supposed conflict will not in fact exist. The widespread opinion that this force normally operates results from the history of the inter-war period which was characterized by under-employment. In times of inflation, on the other hand, all the goods that can be procured can be sold more or less irrespectively of price. The trader's turnover is not limited by the equation of marginal cost and marginal revenue but by the amount of goods he can get to sell (see

Appendix to Chapter III). We should not forget the possibility that the post-war economic climate, in Europe anyhow, may have changed from one of general trade depression and redundant productive capacity typical of the inter-war period, to one of full-employment. There is no guarantee that monopoly powers will be used with equal discretion in a sellers' and in a buyers' market.

What is a Trade Association?

Previous chapters have dealt with organizational features of the distributive trades which are either widely known or can readily be verified by the individual shopper. The present chapter deals with an integral part of the distributive trades' organization which is well concealed from the public view by a silence to which the Press and the professional economist alike have been party. This lack of information is all the more surprising and regrettable in so far as the development of Trade Association activity is the most outstanding change of this century and it is, to an important extent, determining the structure of retail and wholesale trading.

A trade association is a non-profit making organization of enterprises engaged in a particular kind of business and it is normally voluntary. The enterprises may be either individuals, partnerships or corporations and they are normally competitors. Trade Associations now cover the whole field of industry and commerce in this country and in the United States and they are an accepted part of the economic organization in the eyes of industry, trade, the judiciary and the Government. It is therefore surprising at first sight that the general public in Britain, knows little about them and that there should, in fact, be no published list of Trade Associations available to the public.[1]

This seems to be due to the following reasons.

The Trade Associations themselves have nothing to gain by advertising their existence outside the bounds of the particular industry to which their members belong and possibly

[1]The nearest approach to information of this kind, in Britain, would be the Ministry of Labour and National Service, *Directory of Employers Organizations*. American Associations are listed in Temporary National Economic Committee, *Monograph No.* 18, *Trade Association Survey*, Appendix.

to related industries. Accordingly, their activities, in so far as they are reported at all, appear in general only in trade journals. The small distributors in this country have always used their political influence to resist the collection of statistics relating to their industry. A recent illustration is the attitude of the small trader to the proposal made in 1947 to take an official Census of Distribution. The Committee appointed by the Board of Trade to report on the advisability of such a census reported as follows:

"We have had evidence on this subject from 16 Associations speaking mainly on behalf of the medium-sized and smaller type of retailer trader. Some important Associations of this type supported the proposal but others gave views in strong terms against the institution of a census. . . . The main objections can be listed as follows:—

(*a*) that there is anxiety over revealing confidential information about businesses;

(*b*) that the retailer objects strongly to rendering compulsory returns;

(*c*) that the census would lead to a general system of shop licensing;

(*d*) that false conclusions, injurious to trade, would be drawn from the census material;

(*e*) that the cost of a census would be excessive.[1]

Prevailing view that retail trade is competitive

Analytical economists, partly as a result of the lack of handy descriptive material and the complete absence of statistical data and partly as a result of prolonged misapprehension of the character of competition have largely preferred other fields of inquiry. The illusion is thus widespread that retail trading is competitive. The fallacious reasoning underlying this opinion was originally something like the following: concentration of business leading to larger enterprises gives rise to monopoly; the retailer is typically a small man; therefore retail trade is by and large competitive. This syllogism contains the following sources of error: first, while the small, individual shop is still numerically preponderant, the volume of sales by large

[1]Cmd. 6764 (1946) *Report of the Census of Distribution Committee*, 5.

distributive units is at least fifty per cent of the whole; "typically" is thus an ambiguous concept. Secondly, even if the entire volume of retail trade were conducted by small individual retailers, it would not follow that the retail trade was competitive because the retailers might determine their selling policy in association with one another and thus behave as monopolists while remaining very numerous and individually small. It is true that retail distribution is inherently decentralized; some shops will be near consumers and consumers are geographically dispersed. It does not follow from this that retail selling *policy* is also necessarily decentralized. The fact that misunderstanding on this point should have persisted in this country for half a century is attributable in large measure to the lack of factual data on the Trade Associations movement.

Extent of Trade Association

Levy has made extensive investigations in this field. His opinion is "They (Trade Associations) cover the whole field of retail business activities." The "decisive change from competitive to associative organization in almost every trade in Great Britain occurred at the end of the last and the first decades of the new (20th) century".[1] The recent Report on the Working of the Agricultural Marketing Acts[2] refers to the concentration of buying power in wholesale and retail distribution in this country and reflects on the "steady growth of monopolistic combines and practices in industry and trade after the 1914-18 War".

United States

We have a clear picture of the organization in the United States. Trade Association in the United States dates from the Civil War (only two existing Trade Associations date back to before 1860) but was not "industrially widespread" until the 1890s. The period 1890-1915 saw a rapid increase in the number of Associations and in the scope of their activity culminating in the remarkable consolidation of their position

[1]Levy, Retail Trade Association, 20.
[2]Ministry of Agriculture and Fisheries, Economic Series 48 (1947), 5.

in the First World War. Two wars have provided, in both countries, a forcible stimulus to trade association.

The history of the movement shows that Trade Associations flourished in wartime and that industrial depression, falling prices and contracting volume of business provide an uncongenial atmosphere for association in this as in other fields. In the United States, the period of bad trade 1920-4 saw a decrease in the rate of formation of trade associations; in 1925-9 prosperity coincided with a greater rate of formation than ever before; the second post-war slump occasioned an abrupt decline in 1930, '31 and '32. Measures taken by the National Recovery Administration arrested this decline and nearly 23 per cent of the associations now in existence were formed during this administration (1933-5).[1] The stimulus provided by war is both economic and political; total war produces a chronic tendency towards inflation; rising prices increase the order of magnitude of profits including monopoly profits. The plums of association are at such times particularly luscious. Moreover, democratic governments consciously use Trade Associations for the purpose of negotiation with trade and industry. The fact that the retail trade associations typically include no more than some three-quarters of the individual traders among their members and a lesser proportion of retailers has not prevented the adoption of this technique which is, in fact, dictated by convenience rather than ideology. If the Trade Associations are to conduct negotiations with the government on matters intimately affecting, often even directly regulating, the activities of the individual trader, the individual trader's incentive to belong to the association is very much increased. While the Trade Associations have not yet devoted themselves in this country extensively to "public relations" they have learned the necessity for keeping a finger on the governmental pulse. Most important Trade Associations in this country have representatives in London, the home incidentally of a large and important Trade Association "Secretaries' Club". American statistics show that Trade Association headquarters are normally located in the most important commercial or industrial centre for the industry, with the interesting exception of Washington D.C., neither

[1]Temporary National Economic Committee, *Monograph* 18 (1944), 12.

a commercial nor an industrial centre, but the seat of the Federal government, where a large number have their headquarters. A questionnaire circulated to American Associations asking which five types of activity they regarded as their most important revealed that both wholesale and retail associations included "Government Relations."[1]

Organizational Structure of Trade Associations

Bearing in mind that there is almost no generalization which is valid over the whole field of trade association we may proceed to describe certain general characteristics:

Trade Associations both in this country and in the United States normally cover one level of commercial or industrial activity only; thus they are normally either manufacturing, wholesaling or retailing. It is estimated that, in the United States, 6 per cent of the total number of manufacturers' Associations (in 1941) admitted wholesalers and/or retailers as voting members; while 15 per cent of wholesalers' associations and 11 per cent of all associations extended voting to members in other stages of the industrial process. The history of such a remarkable exception as the British Motor Trade Association (see below, p. 163), however, raises the question whether this division is not so much one of Trade Association policy as of the particular stage of development in a progress towards vertical combination of Associations in a given commodity-sector, like automobiles.

Administration is democratic in so far as membership of a given industry or trade is normally the sole qualification for entry but the epithet democratic must be denied to those Associations where membership is made the condition of receiving supplies. Policy is normally determined by a committee of members elected by secret ballot and it appears that membership carries voting rights in the proportion of one vote to each member irrespectively of size. It is impossible to make a satisfactory quantitative estimate of membership in this country but it is estimated[2] that, in the United States, the average number of voting members (which is regarded as

[1]Temporary National Economic Committee, id.
[2]Temporary National Economic Committee, id.

equivalent to the average number of enterprises) was in the period 1937-38, 362 per association but that this was largely an arithmetical concept since widely varying memberships ranged from 106 in manufacturing to 2,417 in retailing and, within the field of retailing itself, membership ranged from as low as ten in the case of mail order houses to 10,000! American statistics indicate that coverage is by no means universal or even, in some cases, extensive and the same is true in this country. The majority of associations in the retail and service industries reported that they included as members less than 50 per cent of the firms in their field—though it is interesting to note that their membership corresponded to more than 50 per cent of the volume of business and Associations with fewest members tended to be the most representative—an indication that it is more difficult to organize large numbers of small people than small numbers of large people. Trustification of an industry would, of course, obviate the necessity for "association."

It seems probable that neither the staffs nor the funds of the majority of Trade Associations are large compared with the resources of the industries concerned. The Associations are usually financed principally by dues paid by all members, sometimes on a flat rate, sometimes according to size; but income is also derived from the sale of publications and the charge for special services provided for members by the association. Figures are available for the United States which suggest that 20 per cent of Trade Associations levied dues on members at a flat rate irrespectively of size while 61 per cent levied dues proportionately to some measure of the size of the business[1]: information on this point was not available for all trade associations.

No comprehensive national organization on a national basis

The Trade Associations in this country are not affiliated to any national body. Levy notes[2] that they frequently find office space and facilities in local Chambers of Commerce to which they are often affiliated. But their relationship to the local Chambers of Commerce is so informal and sporadic that,

[1]Temporary National Economic Committee, id., 11.
[2]Levy, *Trade Association* (1942), 52.

as Levy emphasizes, it could not be deemed in any way equivalent to a national organization. Manufacturers' Associations are, however, frequently affiliated with the Federation of British Industries. The same kind of arrangements prevail in the United States, where some trade associations, but by no means all, are affiliated to the Chamber of Commerce and Manufacturers' Associations with the National Association of Manufacturers.

Trade Association staffs are normally small.[1] It appears that in this country, only in the course of the last war was the keeping of systematic records widely practised and, at the same time, the Associations began to employ professional economists at their headquarters. The extent of the trade associations' activities varies very widely with the particular case. Levy has attempted to clarify the prevailing confusion of ideas on this subject, first by distinguishing associations of producers from associations of traders and restricting the term "trade association" to the latter. It is an important distinction of ideas but it is unlikely that the term trade association will be, in fact, restricted to associations of traders because by custom the phrase is applied also to associations of manufacturers. Secondly, Levy distinguishes those associations of distributors which do and those which do not "attempt to exert a direct influence upon the members' business policy." He argues that the borderline between the two types is "rather shadowy" and points out that the first type may easily develop, in the course of time, into the second. He instances the Retail Distributors' Association, with its excellent research facilities, as an example of the first type but concludes that British trade associations were in the first instance "mostly identified with the control of selling prices" and that "price control . . . tends to overshadow all other association activities."[2]

Trade Association policies
Resale price maintenance

The basis of the Trade Associations' price policy is resale

[1]Private organizations are sometimes employed for particular purposes, for example, for sales promotion.
[2]Levy, id.

price maintenance. The administration of prices in this manner has exercised a profound influence on the organization of the distributive trades in this country and on the cost of distribution. The economic issues involved are discussed in full in Chapters III and IV.

Exchange of information and experience

The Trade Association has other activities more or less associated with price administration. What are these other activities? The personal association of producers or traders in a given field for the purpose of exchanging information and experience; the elimination of competitive antagonism, by the definition of fair trade practices; trade promotion; and government relations and, remarkable concept, "the preservation of competition in its original sense of "to strive together for the common interests."[1] In sum: the aim of association is to better the competitive position of an industry in relation to others and to regulate the play of competition within the industry.

Once the condition of a competitive market is removed, namely, that each producer or trader takes no account of the possible reaction of competitors to changes in his selling behaviour, the emergence of some such type of association is assured (see Chapter III). Trade Associations have come to stay and they have valuable functions to perform.

British Motor Trade Association

In the prevailing absence of information on Trade Association activity a book like *Control in Retail Industry*, written by the Secretary of the Motor Trade Association about the M.T.A. is much to be welcomed. This book gives a clear picture from the inside of the working of the Motor Trade Association, and the controversial character of the writer's thesis which is put forward without debate confirms the view that in trade association circles not only is "the economic necessity for greater control of the competitive forces in modern business"[2] taken as axiomatic but also the more questionable thesis that "competition should be directed to quality and service rather than to price"[3] and that *therefore* resale price maintenance is required.

[1]Temporary National Economic Committee, *Monograph* 18, 47.
[2]Johnson-Davies, *Control in Retail Industry* (1945), 1.
[3]Johnson-Davies, id., 2.

In the words of the author: "It then becomes necessary to ensure that profit *margins* are maintained." It is here that the trade association performs its most useful service, he adds, "by exercising such discipline over the industry as may be reasonably calculated to ensure that the prescribed margin of profit is retained by the dealer, and that the manufacturer's product is not prostituted by price cutting nor prejudiced by price inflation"—These are strong words. They are quoted to emphasize the degree to which Trade Association in this country is, at present, wedded to the policy of resale price maintenance and the reader is again referred to Chapter III for a discussion of the fairly complicated economic issues involved.

The Motor Trade Association is the archetype of trade association in the sense that it covers the entire motor trade, both horizontally and vertically including in its membership all distributors and all producers.[1] It is interesting to discuss its organization and policy in detail because the fundamental economic issues which have confronted this association are those which confront all associations and the particular solutions adopted may become more general.

The origin of the Motor Trade Association illustrates the important interest of manufacturers, once large-scale production is undertaken, in efficient distribution of their product. The Motor Trade Association is a trade union (see above, p. 148) combining car manufacturer members who also belong to the Society of Motor Manufacturers and Traders, Ltd., and distributors who also belong, for the most part, to the Motor Agents' Association, Ltd. The first association in the motor industry was formed by *manufacturers* to solve a distribution problem: sizeable discounts (i.e. the difference between their buying and selling price which, after allowance for operative costs, constitutes the distributor's profits) were allowed to traders selling new cars because the costs of efficient distribution were high. The distribution of motor-cars is a skilled business involving capital investment in substantial premises and technical knowledge on the part of the distributor since the

[1]"The membership includes, without exception, all manufacturers and concessionaires of motor cars marketed in Great Britain and their respective wholesale and retail dsitributors and dealers." Johnson-Davies, id., 12.

servicing of a car is an important factor in determining the efficiency of its performance.

The distribution problem confronting manufacturers was as follows. The margin allowed by the manufacturers to traders had attracted a "multitude of unskilled showmen" who proceeded to exhibit cars all over the country and after making immediate profits, as often as not, abandoned the trade. The S.M.M. and T. put a stop to this by the simple expedient of associating manufacturers in an engagement to deny supplies to all such wildcat tradesmen on pain of forfeiting their Bond to the association. The particular interest of both parties is clear: the manufacturers required efficient distribution; since the distribution of motor-cars is necessarily a costly business and, for its proper performance, requires an initial investment by the retailer, the manufacturer had to prevent "cut-throat" competition from providing a disincentive to legitimate (i.e. efficient) traders. The legitimate traders' interest was clearly in the prevention of undercutting. The public's interest was in efficient distribution and servicing and uninterrupted manufacture: it thus required *some* "regulation" of competition in the field of manufacture and distribution.

Regulation has, in practice, taken the form of the complete proscription of price-competition among distributors. To secure this a rigid control has been established over the "allowance" which dealers may make for a used-car turned in in part exchange. "Some 90 per cent of new car sales involve the part-exchange of a used car"[1]—an easy way of cutting prices was then to increase the allowance on used cars. This was widely done. The problem presented itself at first to all parties in the industry, as a purely distributive problem, viz. one trader stealing customers from another; the manufacturers accordingly stood aloof and the traders established an "Agents Section" of the S.M.M. & T. to deal with the problem. Johnson-Davies writes that so long as the manufacturers did no more than lend the Association their passive support the used car problem became continually more acute. The legitimate agents' stocks of used cars rapidly increased and absorbed continually more capital. Financial mortality among distribu-

[1]Johnson-Davies, id., 14.

tive traders was high. Returns on invested capital were so low as not to attract further capital. Public service was prejudiced.[1] Retailers showed in 1935 estimated losses on used cars exchanged for new cars to the tune of some £4,000,000 per annum. Accordingly, in 1935, the Motor Trade Association was reconstituted and became a manufacturer-controlled association. "Dealer membership was made a condition of being granted trade terms on cars."[2] A complete monopoly in the domestic production and sale of cars had thus been established; manufacturers are guarded from foreign competition by the requirement of an import licence and an allocation of foreign exchange.

Johnson-Davies describes policy in the Motor Trade Association as made by the President and a Council of thirty-six members, mainly manufacturers but including traders, elected by their representative groups. Day to day administration of the Motor Trade Association Rules is the affair of the secretary assisted by a staff of permanent officials organized into the following departments: General Administration; Statistical; Judicial; Inspection; Trade Relations.

Thus a complete monopoly of domestic production and distribution in an essential industry has been established by the instrument of the Trade Association. Commercial policy is determined by the manufacturers without any public supervision whatsoever. This monopoly openly uses the sanction of boycott to enforce its authority. *Any* instance of price competition exposes the trader to inclusion in the "Stop List" of traders who are boycotted by the entire industry and are thus denied supplies; "on the inclusion of the name of a given person in the Stop List of the Motor Trade Association, manufacturers, distributors and factors immediately cease supplies of cars and other motor trade goods[3]. . . . An effective observance of a Stop List leading to an immediate cessation of the wherewithal to trade, must clearly result in the commercial extinction of a firm whose name is published thereon." The Motor Trade[4] Association's actions have been upheld in the courts; in the present state of the law they are entirely legal. So much for the common law doctrine of "restraint of trade."

[1]Johnson-Davies, id., 14.
[2]Johnson-Davies, id., 12.
[3]Johnson-Davies, id., 27.
[4]Johnson-Davies, id., 28.

Meaning of Restraint of Trade

They are held to be legitimate because of their economic justification. It is a paradoxical situation which places on the shoulders of the judiciary economic issues which are among the most complicated and which can only be defined and resolved with the aid of the most recently devised analytical tools. Surely government should take the responsibility for the determination of public policy by legislation and the judiciary for interpreting the law. The important issues concerning *public* policy are the practice of resale price maintenance in particular and trade association policy in general.

Four important reasons have been given why large-scale producers have an interest in minimizing price fluctuations.[1] In so far as the manufacturers' interest is the reduction of production costs, as in the case of efficient cost accounting, it coincides with that of the community. The identity of interest between manufacturer and consumer is not, however, so clear in the following respects. Likely corollaries of price stability as an act of managerial discretion, are:

The corollaries of price maintenance

(*a*) an increased concentration on the quality and performance of the product as opposed to price appeal;

(*b*) a decreased attention to the invention of cheaper lines for their own sake. These tendencies are widely illustrated by our own experience (automobile production is an excellent example), and by American experience.[2] Increased concentration on the quality and performance of the product has certain obvious merits from the consumers' point of view, in the perfection of the article.

Are they in the public interest?

The decreased attention to the invention of cheaper lines would be reduced if monopoly in the field of production were sufficiently controlled to allow the entry of new firms manufacturing lines which would satisfy hitherto unsatisfied demands. It is difficult to resist the conclusion of the Temporary National

[1] 14f. above.

[2] cf. Temporary National Economic Committee, Monograph No. 1, *Price Behaviour and Business Policy passim.*

Economic Committee on the Concentration of Economic Power that the "basic solution of curtailed production for selfish ends is to be found . . . in the development of competing, industries and firms."

As far as the producer is concerned, price stability as such, taking no account for the time being of the methods by which that stability is secured, must be considered an advantage.

It must be admitted, however, that when manufacturers choose to compete by differentiating products instead of reducing prices, the consumer's problem of choice from a variety of merchandise is thereby complicated. Price is a readily understood measure of relative values. "The translation of collateral terms of sale to price equivalents is difficult for the average untrained consumer. It is questionable, however, whether the final consumer, as contrasted with the trader, because of the severe limits imposed by distance on his knowledge of market conditions, has ever been a powerful agent in the comparison of market values other than those presented to him in his immediate geographical neighbourhood through the organization of the distributive trades. In this case, we presume a certain technical knowledge on the part of trade buyers, the comparison of collateral terms of sale should not be much less effective than the price differential."[1]

Price maintenance has certain economic advantages

Price maintenance then in and by itself might conceivably have greater economic advantages than demerits.

Importance of the means by which it is effected

It is the means by which price-maintenance is secured that may, as indeed in the United Kingdom and in the United States it is in process of doing, (*a*) sterilize industrial and commercial enterprise, and (*b*) lead to an over-expansion of the distributive trades as a whole and the "freezing" of what should be the developing technology of the distributive trades.

Where price stability is achieved by agreement among producers and/or traders with a view to resale price maintenance, the forces making for economic, low-cost, production and

[1]Temporary National Economic Committee, No. 18.

distribution are paralysed. What we are now confronted with is, in effect, stabilization or fixity in distributive margins or relative prices at the production, wholesale and retail level, determined most often by associated manufacturers and distributors in agreement and enforced by the method of boycott.

Resale price maintenance removes, by the sanction of suppliers' boycott, the possibility of retailers' competing, in the sale of price-maintained goods, by means of reducing prices. The competitive weapons they use in preference are likely to involve an increase in selling costs. The consumer meets these costs in the price he pays for the product.

The second point of major importance in connection with distributive margins under price maintenance is that where distributors are of different efficiency (have different average costs), all but the least efficient will show varying degrees of differential profit. Negotiated prices are unlikely to be lower than the costs of the *marginal* (or least efficient) distributor. This will provide an expansionist influence. Where profits appear to be high, new-comers will enter. The administration of negotiated prices, fixed necessarily for political reasons at a level which will cover marginal costs, will provide a never-ending stimulus to expansion in the distributive trades. Additional shops will squeeze in among existing ones and new retail prices and margins will be arranged to cover the new and increased average costs resulting from decreased turnover and increased selling costs where over-expansion has taken place; traders will argue (rightly) that they could not "make ends meet" on the existing margins.

Resale price maintenance exaggerates the tendency to over-expansion of the distributive trades

Where there is no limitation on entry into the retail distributive trades, because of the imperfectly competitive character of the market, there will be a chronic tendency for "too many" people to become shopkeepers and, correspondingly, for the size of the average firm to be "too small".[1] Resale price-

[1]Lerner and Singer, *Journal of Political Economy* (April, 1937).
Lewis, *Economica* (November, 1945) "Competition in Retail Trade," 202.

maintenance exaggerates this *uneconomic* tendency. (v. Chapter II, p. 28f). These terms mean nothing unless they are related to some criterion with respect to which they are too numerous and too small. The criterion we shall choose is the same that the ordinary man chooses to determine the appropriateness of his economic actions, namely, do they satisfy his wants with the least expenditure of the resources at his disposal as represented by his income. As far as the aggregate of shoppers is concerned, the expenditure of resources involved in retail distribution can be divided into two groups—retailers' costs, plus the cost of transport borne by the customers. The costs sustained by the customer include not only the bus fare or shoe leather spent on covering the distance between home and shop, but also the nuisance of interrupting other jobs to go shopping, of sitting in crowded buses, and so on.

Where retail price maintenance is practised, the tendency which in all cases exists towards an uneconomically large number of retail stores, is very much increased. Traders' costs are thereby increased. This might be considered a legitimate increase in traders' costs if it could be shown that it was more than compensated for by the consequent reduction in transport costs borne by the consumer. But the practice of resale price maintenance *prevents* the consumer from demonstrating his preference. The condemnation of resale price maintenance is made all the stronger by reference to the grave limitation it imposes on the consumer's freedom of choice.

Resale price maintenance limits the shopper's freedom of choice

One of the principles underlying democracy is that only those limitations on the consumer's freedom of choice should be imposed which secure a more than countervailing benefit. The only justification of the heavy cost of distributive services which we pay to-day would be that it provided the mechanism for the exercise of consumer's choice, whether by allowing the consumer to delegate the selection of merchandise to the shopkeeper, or by presenting the customer with a wide range of merchandise from which to choose.

The conclusion reached as the result of the above analysis is that the retail market is characteristically and inevitably imperfectly competitive. Consumers are geographically dispersed and they *prefer* various types of retail service to others. These are the facts of life. The economic theorist cannot alter them; his responsibility is to note their existence and to identify the results to which they give rise.

If resale price maintenance is contrary to the interests of the consumers, tends to favour and keep alive inefficient distributors in the face of over-capacity of the industry as a whole, to discriminate against the introduction of new and more efficient techniques of distribution and to prevent the consumer from exercising a choice between more elaborate distributive services and lower prices, it follows that something should be done to arrest its spread.

CHAPTER IX

WAR AND POST-WAR PROBLEMS

WARTIME experience provides one further important source of information and enlightenment which we have not yet considered. Most of the investigation so far has been based on peacetime experience because it has been assumed that democratic communities do not wish to adopt, in peacetime, the totalitarian methods of control suitable to the conduct of total war. Though many of the wartime controls will doubtless remain, several important controls like the direction of labour and the licensing of entry in retail distribution have in principle been rejected and in practice substantially[1] removed. It is assumed that whatever solution is found must be found within the democratic framework.

Wartime experience

War provides a laboratory in which the economic processes at work are selected for critical examination in a manner which is not customary in a democratic state in peacetime. Furthermore, the controls imposed to achieve a variety of wartime ends, exercise a lasting effect on the organization of industry and trade. So it was with the distributive trades. When the war came to an end, we did not immediately resume the marketing methods of 1939.

Some of the controls affecting shop-keeping were, indeed, removed; but we should not therefore expect the methods of distribution in 1948 to be unchanged in comparison with those of 1939.

[1]"Direction" of labour was brought to an end in 1946 and the Control of Engagement Order, requiring unemployed in various categories to obtain employment through a labour exchange and imposing a similar requirement on employers, was reintroduced in 1947.But this measure affects only those who are seeking employment and does not provide for the direction of those, who are already at work. Under full employment, this measure cannot be held to affect the pattern of labour distribution to any important extent. In January 1946, the Location of Retail Business Orders, limiting entry into the non-food retail trade were revoked. Licensing of the retail sale of food continues.

Wartime controls affecting distribution

In face of the variety of types of wholesale and retail businesses and of the variety of conditions ruling in different geographical areas (owing to factors like evacuation of population from bombed areas and the strategy of war production) there were no obvious lines which nation-wide control of distribution could take. The technique of wartime control was to institute specific controls for urgent purposes like the mobilization of labour for the armed forces; consumer rationing to secure the equitable distribution of limited supplies; price control to prevent progressive inflation; and raw material controls to reserve essential materials for war production. Shop-keepers were very much affected by these controls. Their labour was called up, their sales were subjected to price and rationing regulations and their day-to-day operations were affected by a variety of "austerity" regulations designed to economize such things as paper and petrol.

Controls limiting the availability of consumers' goods

The principal controls affecting shop-keepers were as follows: as the mobilization for war proceeded, men who formerly produced food and household goods, were taken either into the armed forces or into the munitions industries. It is estimated that the volume of goods being sold at retail decreased, from 1938 to 1941, by between 15 and 20 per cent, and, during the remaining years of the war remained slightly below the 1941 level. [1]

This contraction was largely sustained in the supply of consumers' goods, other than food. Whereas the annual *per capita* consumption of food[2] decreased by 11 per cent, between the outbreak of war and 1941, the decrease in the volume of civilian clothing supplies during the same period is estimated at 38 per cent, for men's and boys' clothing and at 41 per cent for women's and children's clothing. The years 1941-4 showed a slight increase in the availability of supplies (following Lend-Lease) but 1944, compared with 1938, showed a net decrease of 35 per cent in men's and boys' clothing and a decrease of 39 per cent in women's and children's clothing.

[1]Report of the Combined Production and Resources Board.
[2]Valued at pre-war prices to give an index of volume.

The obvious method of reducing civilian consumption would be the imposition of consumer rationing, which in its various forms, is a sufficiently fine instrument of control to secure the maximum of consumers' choice, both of commodities and salesmen, consistent with any required reduction in aggregate consumption. Under rationing, the consumer is free (within limitations imposed by registration requirements) to shop where he chooses and the maximum freedom is afforded the retailer to obtain his supplies where he will. This freedom of choice provides a stimulus towards the provision of efficient retailing and wholesaling services. Coupons flow backwards from consumers via traders to manufacturers as supplies flow forwards, acting much in the manner of a second currency and, like currency, in principle without effect on the channels of trade. In practice, however, the characteristic imperfections of the retail market were once again evidenced even in the rationing system. Registration (whereby shoppers were required to restrict their custom to a given retailer) was required for the basic foodstuffs. By this means, the supplies in the distributive pipeline required to guarantee consumers' rations at all times and places were reduced to a minimum, because the pattern of consumers' purchases was stabilized and it was, therefore known how much of these basic foods would be required in any area at any time. Traders tended to sell the unrationed goods as a means of inducing and retaining registrations—a form of non-price competition—and consumers accordingly showed a preference for registering for the basic foodstuffs with a shop which stocked a variety of unrationed goods. Registration for the basic foods thus discriminated, prior to the institution of points rationing of the majority of other foods (after December, 1941), against traders specializing in a narrow range of goods.[1]

[1]The *Annual Report* of the Maypole Dairy Co., Ltd., for May, 1942, reads as follows: "General grocery goods were in increasingly short supply and retailers, in many instances, adopted the practice of refusing to sell these goods except to customers who were registered with them for rationed articles. This practice was actually encouraged by the Ministry of Food and indeed was not unreasonable since it helped shopkeepers to control the distribution of these unrationed goods. . . . the effect, however, on our company, which specializes in butter, margarine and eggs, etc., as opposed to general grocery stocks, was that the number of our customers who used to come to us especially for butter, margarine, eggs, etc., found themselves forced to register with general grocers in order to get other goods. The introduction

Statistics recently published by the Ministry of Food show that an increased proportion of registrations for sugar, for fats and for bacon (1940-6) went to independent traders, in spite of the fact that the number of independents decreased because both multiple shops and co-operatives had each bought up some five hundred independent stores (0.2 per cent of the total number).[1] This practice discriminated against the shop which specialized in a small range of products, as for instance, the multiple shops. It can, however, be said that by and large, consumer rationing was the fairest means of limiting supplies of consumers' goods both as between traders and as between consumers, and it should be observed that rationing regulations covered a far higher proportion—some 75 per cent—of expenditure on food than on non-food consumables.[2]

The operation of consumer rationing is, however, a huge administrative task[3] and it was preceded and supplemented by other forms of control which also had a pronounced effect on the structure of trade. The main ones were as follows:

Raw materials controls

(*a*) From the outbreak of war raw materials controls secured the allocation of sufficient quantities of the basic materials of industry to the military sector and to the production of minimum civilian requirements. These controls affected traders for the most part only indirectly.

Limitation of Supplies Orders

(*b*) Limitation of Supplies Orders, starting in the spring of 1940, restricted by quota, supplies of consumers' goods

[1]See Appendix 1.

[2]Consumer rationing of clothing and footwear, on the points system, was introduced in May, 1941. Consumer rationing of bacon and ham, butter and sugar was introduced in January 1940, and of meat in March, 1940. A points rationing system of tinned foods and cereals was introduced after December, 1941.

[3]It was estimated that, by 1942, there were 1,500 Local Food Offices.

of the points rationing system to a large range of previously unrationed articles removed to a large extent the difficulties in which our customers were placed and has contributed to the development of our trade in the articles affected. We, therefore, welcomed this new feature in the rationing methods employed by the Ministry of Food and we think that it is generally agreed that it has done much to ensure fairer distribution of unrationed goods."

(other than food) by any manufacturer or wholesaler to retailers to a percentage of the value of their sales in a standard period, April-September, 1939 for clothing and December, 1939-May, 1940, for miscellaneous goods. Supplies under these orders were, in the course of the next twelve months, reduced to anything from one-third to two-thirds of the *value* of the sales in the standard period which meant an even greater reduction in quantity. Within these quotas suppliers to the retail level were free to sell to whomever they wished: retailers under this sytem, unlike the rationing system, had no claim to scarce supplies but became dependent on the goodwill of the wholesaler or manufacturer. The tendency under such a system was to "play safe", to keep traditional contacts with a view not only to the current but to the post-war position. It militated in favour of existing arrangements and against innovation. It thus helped to confirm an evil tendency already manifest in the 1930s.

When, in spite of this tendency, the progressive contractions of supplies in the non-food sector disclosed the far greater mortality of the small-scale than the large-scale trader, the so-called Fair Shares[1] scheme was introduced with the aim of guaranteeing, in so far as this was possible, a share of supplies to the small trader which should correspond to his pre-war (not his current) proportion of the trade. From that time on, the Government's policy was one of protecting existing trading interests in the pre-war pattern.

Price control

War involves a severe reduction in the volume of goods for sale and at the same time an increase in the amount of money

[1]In October, 1942, the President of the Board of Trade announced a new programme of control directed at securing a fair share of supplies to small retailers by guaranteeing them a minimum quota of available goods, particularly in areas where population had increased from wartime causes. Any retailers having total sales not exceeding £5,000 a year for clothing, £2,500 for hollow-ware and £3,000 for pottery were eligible for inclusion in the scheme. Suppliers to the retail level were directed to provide each of these eligible retail customers with a *minimum* proportion of the goods supplied him *in a standard year*.

people have to spend as a result of higher rates of pay and fuller employment: unemployment disappears and overtime is widespread. This situation gives rise to the so-called inflationary gap: too much money running after too few goods. The danger of inflation is epidemic in wartime. As all prices are part of someone else's costs and as everyone endeavours to cover his costs by increasing his prices (whether the prices of the goods he is marketing or of his own labour) wartime governments normally intervene to arrest an inflationary spiral of prices and try to stabilize prices by administrative action.

The government's wartime price policies were based at any rate, until September, 1941, on the same principle—to maintain traders' net profits at pre-war levels. The utility programme for the manufacture of standardized articles after late 1941 facilitated an important change in this technique of price control in the field of utility goods.

The story of wartime price administration in Britain is complicated by the particular administrative arrangements in Whitehall whereby the authority of particular Departments of State is determined by reference not to a particular administrative function but a particular commodity. Thus the Ministry of Food deals with food while the Board of Trade is the department responsible for the government regulation—either price control or rationing or whatever other form of control—of non-food consumers' goods. The Ministry of Agriculture and Fisheries deals with agriculture and fisheries, the Ministry of Fuel and Power with fuel and power. This helps to explain why the techniques of control differed in the different commodity sectors but it makes the story somewhat more difficult to tell in brief.

Prices of Goods Act

Price control over the non-food articles was originally administered under the Prices of Goods Act (2 and 3 George VI, Ch. 118) passed on the outbreak of war (Sept., 1939). The method of control under this Act is of some importance to an understanding of the impact of war experience on traders in this field. The primary purpose of the Act was to prevent profiteering rather than to prevent price increases. The law prohibited the sale of goods at any price exceeding the "permitted" price, viz. the "basic" price plus any permitted increase". The basic price for any particular commodity was the price for that commodity which prevailed on 21st August, 1939. Increases were, however, permitted to cover any legitimate increase in costs and this was taken to include *increased incidence of overhead costs* resulting from diminished turnover.

In July, 1940, the Central Price Regulation Committee adopted a formula by which retailers could compute permitted prices.

The method of calculation is illustrated in the following example:

Consider a business whose pre-war expenses were 25 per cent of the volume of sales and whose expenses have now risen to 30 per cent of the volume of sales, perhaps a result of reduced turnover. If the pre-war cost price of the article in question was 10/- and the pre-war selling price was 13/4 but the trader has now to pay not 10/- but 12/- cost price, then the present permitted price of the article would be calculated as follows:

	s.	*d.*
(*a*) Pre-war selling price	13	4
(*b*) Increase in cost price	2	0
(*c*) *Add* (*b*) a margin of 25 per cent (i.e. pre-war expense ratio of the business) on returns[1] ..	0	8
(*d*) Total of (*b*) and (*c*)	2	8
(*e*) Total of (*a*) and (*d*)	16	0
(*f*) *Add* to (*e*) a further margin of 5 per cent on returns (i.e. the increase in the expense ratio of the business) .. .. .. (approx.)	0	10
Permitted price ..	16	10

The extent of the permitted increase in price depended, first, on the increase in cost price and, second, on the increase in expense ratio. The first removed the retailer's incentive to buy in the cheapest market because his percentage mark-up

[1]That is 33⅓ per cent. on the increment of cost. (A mark-up of 25 per cent on returns is the equivalent of 33⅓ per cent on cost.).

was computed on a greater total sum if he paid a higher price. The second reduced his incentive to run his business efficiently: if his expense ratio increased, he was permitted a higher mark-up. For those types of trading unit whose main appeal to the consumer was not, in any case, a price appeal[1] this method of price control was an invitation to high cost operation and inefficiency. The non-availability of supplies limited the extent to which those traders whose main appeal was a price appeal could take advantage of price differentials.

Goods and Services (Price Control) Act

Since July, 1941, however, this form of price control of non-food consumers' goods has been progressively replaced by a different technique of control under the Goods and Services (Price Control) Act.[2] Under the Supplementary Act, specific maximum prices (price ceilings) and maximum margins were determined for each controlled commodity. The new technique of price control was associated with the new policy (beginning mid-1941) of standardizing production in "utility" lines. Overall price ceilings could not be imposed on a heterogeneous mass of commodities; a dramatic illustration of the difficulties of defining commodities and markets.[3] Maximum prices and margins were determined for standardized utility lines in the manner illustrated in the following table:

TABLE VIII

United Kingdom: Price Control of Standardized (Utility) Articles by Maximum Prices and Maximum Margins

I Description of garment	II Manufacturer's net margin of profit (per cent)	III Wholesaler's maximum margin (per cent)	IV Manufacturer's or wholesaler's overriding maximum	V Retailer's maximum margin	VI Retailer's overriding maximum (Purchase tax chargeable)
Youths' suits	4	20	55/-	33⅓	85/7
Men's overcoats	4	20	57/6	33⅓	89/5
Men's trousers	4	20	12/8	33⅓	19/8

Source: Statutory Rule and Order, 1941, 1386

[1]v. Chapters III and IV above.

[2]Goods and Services (Price Control) Act, 1941, 4 and 5 Geo. VI. Ch. 31.

[3]See 38ff above.

The maximum mark-up was a welcome innovation designed to secure that the benefit of lower distribution costs should be passed on to the consumer. But it reduced the incentive to buy cheaply, and all maximum prices and mark-ups, in conditions of inflation (the only conditions in which they are likely to be imposed) tend to become minima.

The administration of food prices on the other hand was from the beginning operated almost entirely on the principle of maximum prices for given commodities. The maximum prices appear to have been calculated on the basis of distributors' costs plus pre-war net profit.[1] This policy was clearly designed to maintain existing trade channels and to avoid widespread insolvency among traders and had some justification in the paramount wartime necessity for keeping open a wide geographical dispersion of food outlets. This was a military necessity. Much has been said about the Ministry of Food being a "distributors ministry"[2] the implication being that the Ministry of Food's margins were over-generous. It would seem nearer the point to say that the administration of any *uniform* retail price will necessarily provide all distributors except those with highest costs with abnormal profits.[3] When supplies are rationed, and therefore scarce there is no incentive to sell down to cost: better than marginal traders can sell all they can get with abnormal profits (v. Chapter III). Abnormal gains will accrue to traders who are nearer the sources of supply and whose transport costs are lower; who provide fewer distributive services: who have a quick turnover and so on. Where it could define the occasion of these abnormal profits, as in our first instance, the Ministry of Food made arrangements for a range of maximum prices according to geographical position[4] (the

[1]Hansard, July 19, 1947. The Minister of Food stated, "We do not fix margins on a percentage basis since this would give a disproportionate increase in net profits when prices have to be raised. Our policy is to adjust pre-war margins to allow for changes in costs, including any expenses which vary with the price of goods. I have no reason to doubt that the average grocer is at least as prosperous now as before the war, but we are, of course, always ready to consider any representations from the trade on the adequacy of margins or profit levels."

[2]cf. Ministry of Agriculture and Fisheries, *Economic Series* 48, (1947).

[3]The "quasi-rent" of Marshalian Theory.

[4]e.g. Potatoes for a period.

maximum price for those nearer the sources of supply being fixed at a lower level than the ceiling for those with higher transport costs); in some cases the Ministry itself paid the transport costs;[1] or again in others transport costs at wholesale were pooled.[2] Where the origin of the differential costs was not so readily determined, as was the case with distributors' operating costs[3] no such correction was possible. The result of price administration of this kind was to prevent the benefits of lower cost distribution from being passed on to the consumer in the form of lower retail prices and further to accustom traders to a regime of fixed prices.

Conscription of labour

The call-up of labour to the armed forces created a further powerful influence on distributive traders. Here again the impact was uneven. Food distributors were more leniently treated than the non-food traders. Furthermore, as between trades, the greater liability to call-up of male[4] as compared with female employees and of salespeople as compared with proprietors and managers discriminated in favour of those industries, which employed a high proportion[5] of female to male labour and those industries where the proportion of proprietors and salespeople was high relatively to employees. This last proportion appears to be at the highest in general and mixed businesses, less markedly so with tobacco and stationery than in other trades and at its lowest in clothing, footwear and drugs.[6]

One deduction must be made from these facts: retail trade is so heterogeneous, that any form of control discriminates

[1]e.g. Fish.

[2]e.g. Meat.

[3]Hansard, July 16, 1947: "With the present methods of marketing and grading it would be impossible to obtain any useful information about profits at any given stage of distribution."

[4]Men were called up between the ages of 19 and 50 and the women between the ages of 20 and 30.

[5]"The relative proportion of females and males engaged in the non-food retail trades differs very widely. In the clothing trades nearly twice as many females as males are engaged. At the other extreme, the furniture and ironmongery trades between them give more than four times as much employment to males as females." (Board of Trade, Retail Trade Committee, *2nd Interim Report*, Appendix p. 4).

[6]Retail Trade Committee, id.

against one type of trading unit or another: yet, owing to the imperfectly competitive character of the market, at wholesale and retail, the results of *laisser faire* on the part of the government would probably, on the basis of pre-war experience, prove to be the most discriminating of all.

Particularly important and indicative in this connection is the position of the co-operative societies. The extent of co-operative trading in the United Kingdom is wide. It is roughly true to say that in every second household in the country at least one person is a member. Yet there is no doubt that the expansion of co-operative trading was held in check, pre-war, by the use of certain restrictive business practices, for example resale price maintenance, by the non-co-operative business world. The payment of a dividend on purchases by co-operative societies is considered by many Trade Associations to be equivalent to a reduction of price. The associations therefore withheld supplies from the co-operatives. The question arises whether such restriction are in the public interest. No one can deny that they are of great importance. Neither the Government nor the public can afford to overlook them in the hope that lack of knowledge excuses inaction and that failure to regulate this battle of the trading types according to the rules of war or of competition constitutes neutrality. There is equally no doubt that wartime regulation has had the effect of limiting the expansion of co-operative trading by tending to preserve the *status quo*.

Yet perhaps, the experience of co-operative trading provides a clue to the solution of some of the problems of the economics of distribution outlined above. In any case, the consumer should not be prevented from arbitrating in this battle between the types of trading unit by regulations either privately or publicly inspired, which are, *de facto*, in restraint of trade.

We referred above to the natural antipathy and suspicion between buyer and seller as being, in some sense, an impediment to the proper performance of the distributive function of interpreting consumers' wants to producers, who are necessarily, once production is on a large scale, widely separated from them. Ideally, the co-operative movement overcomes this suspicion and source of waste by putting the trader in a "fiduciary relationship to the consumer".[1] It is true, that the present practice of co-operative management tends to resemble non-co-operative practice in preferring an increase in the trading surplus to a reduction of prices. In so far as this is done, it is an apparent betrayal of the fiduciary relationship, unless the society members have chosen that their society should be primarily a co-operative saving rather than a co-operative trading society. It is an interesting speculation, how far this tendency is dictated by the practical dangers of retaliation, which would attend a more open threat to existing business practices and which more active price competition on the part of the co-operatives would present. Perhaps this is yet another victory for the forces militating against any disturbance of existing conditions.

Apart from the fiduciary relationship between buyer and seller, which underlies co-operative trading, the experience of co-operative societies is important also from the purely technical standpoint. It is clear that the costs of co-operative distribution are in general lower than those of private traders. They are not of course universally so. The authoritative statement has been made that "Co-operative retail organization appears to effect economies as against all capitalist organization on the score of administration and advertising; as against independent capitalistic shopkeepers and department stores (but not chain stores) on the score of collections of debt and delivery; and as against department stores on the score of rent. . . . Possibly most important is the reduction in the cost of finance."[2] In some cases these economies are achieved at the expense of retail services; those who enjoy elaborate service will shop elsewhere. But this is not the whole story. The conclusion is inescapable that some appreciable economies are achieved by co-operative societies as a result of removing, within the field of co-operative trading, the forces of imperfect competition which, it has been shown above, lead to the spurious multiplication of distributive services by large-scale traders

[1]Smith, *Retail Distribution*, 2nd Edition, 1948, page 217.
[2]Carr Saunders, Florence and Peers, *Consumers' Co-operation in Great Britain*, 3 (1942). See also Appendix III.

as a means of expanding or retaining markets, and that this in turn leads to maintaining prices at a level which provides small traders at a simpler level with some sort of living. The co-operatives' practice of sharing markets—no co-operative will set up nearer than a certain distance to any other—shows that the elimination of these forces by agreement among private traders rather than by government action on behalf of the community would be dangerous indeed. Could means be found of reducing their impact, distribution costs could be reduced. In the field of co-operation, the "fiduciary relationship" of buyer and seller secures that even if the benefits of low costs are not passed on to the consumer in the form of lower prices, they are passed on in the form of dividends.

Wartime control of wholesale trading

Wholesale trade in non-food consumers' goods was affected by the controls outlined earlier in this Chapter. The wholesale trade in food was more directly controlled.

This was for a variety of reasons; the Ministry of Food became itself the sole importer of food on the outbreak of war; commercial importers acted as agents of the Government which by this means was able to prevent the exit of supplies to the black market. With regard to domestic production a variety of particular schemes were brought into operation. Wholesalers were persuaded by the Ministry to form wartime organizations for the combined approach to their problems. In the case of meat, the wholesale trade was even nationalized. But the serious feature of this piecemeal treatment was that no plan for the rationalization of wholesale trade in food as a whole was discernible. On the contrary, the attempt was made to maintain existing trade channels. Some of them were emptied of supplies to economize transport or other scarce resources but the channels were maintained and traders were compensated by their industry. Outstanding cases of the maintenance of redundant traders have several times been brought to the notice of the House of Commons now that distribution problems are coming to the fore. The story is told of meat wholesalers who, now that the wholesale trade in meat has been entrusted to a public body,[1] have lost their pre-war functions

[1]The Wholesale Meat Suppliers' Association.

and are nevertheless still in receipt of annual payments equivalent to 1¾ per cent. on their 1938 turnover from the Wholesale Meat Suppliers' Association.[1] These payments constitute distribution costs and increase the level of subsidies necessary to maintain meat prices at the desired level. Since a turnover of £50,000 a year was by no means unusual, the wholesaler may now be in receipt of £1,000 a year for no work, simply in virtue of his 1938 trade!

It is time that these wartime anomalies were removed. The adjustment of margins policies is admittedly a complicated problem; the same cannot be said of requiring payments to be made to distributors only for services rendered. In 1947 the Ministry of Food promised[2] a reorganization of the system of food distribution. When it implements this promise, a system should be found which places rewards in the way of efficient distributors and penalties for those who commit abuses for which the present system is a breeding place.[3]

It is difficult to resist the conclusion that the war guaranteed pre-war profits of every vested interest in the distributive trades so far as food was concerned.[4] Reconstruction requires the replacement of wartime improvisations by a sounder system. An examination of the pre-war arrangements forbids the conclusion that *laisser-faire* would provide the solution.[5]

The record of wartime experience has, so far, been of negative rather than positive importance in relation to current problems; a cautionary tale: what not to do rather than what to do. It has a further page to contribute which is of considerable relevance to our present problems.

[1]Hansard, June 27, 1947.

[2]Hansard, July 16, 1947, col. 912: "A reorganization of the system of distribution is about to take place in collaboration with the Ministry of Agriculture."

[3]Hansard, July 1, 1947, col. 1180 "It is a semi-monopolistic position in which, whether they like it or not, many traders are placed to-day. It is the breeding ground of these abuses which I do not say for one moment have been indulged in by the majority of traders but which, undoubtedly, have existed in the markets."

[4]Hansard, July 16, 1947, col. 904.

[5]Hansard, June 27 (1947) col. 902. A spokesman in the debate on Food Distribution costs, with twenty-five years' experience of the distributive trades, expressed the view that "Before the war it was a case of private enterprise run riot." Another spokesman referred to the "chaotic laisser-faire system of distribution that applied before the war."

Proposal to concentrate retail trade

Recurrant economic crises in Britain are simply prolongations of wartime troubles: it is the problem of an unaccustomed national poverty with this difference: that during the war people accepted the truth of the position whereas now they are concerned to deny it. The fundamental aim of wartime economic policy was expressed by the President of the Board of Trade in the following terms:

"The fullest possible transfer of resources to war production while maintaining exports as far as practicable. . . . This policy demands the severe cutting down of civil consumption and the release of labour, materials and factory space for more essential services. If they consulted their own interests, the industries concerned might wish that all their component firms should carry on with their remaining share of the trade in the hope that conditions might improve. From the point of view of the national interest, however, it is most undesirable that the reduced production of goods for civil needs should be met by large-scale part-time working . . . a spread over of this kind results in an uneconomical use of certain kinds of labour . . . the effect of a diminished turnover on costs may, in some instances, have serious repercussions on prices. . . ."[1]

The proposal was therefore made by the Board of Trade's Retail Trade Committee for the "concentration" of non-food retail trades by the voluntary withdrawal from business of the shopkeepers who had been hardest hit. It was proposed to assist these temporary withdrawals by compensation payments from a central fund. The fund was to be financed by a compulsory levy of 1 per cent on the turnover of the retail distributors remaining in business to provide a compensation payment of 5 per cent of the retiring traders' turnover for the twelve months prior to their withdrawal from business.[2]

The unanimous opposition by all sections of the trade which greeted these proposals must be interpreted in the light of statistics of wartime mortality[3] of retail traders. (Wartime mortality data on the wholesale trade are not available.)

[1]Cmd. 6258 (1941). Concentration of Production, 2.
[2]Retail Trade Committee, *Third Report*, 1942.
[3]See Appendix IV.

The large-scale retail units showed far greater powers of survival in the face of wartime contractions of business. Confident in their own power of remaining in business, they naturally opposed a scheme which would require them to contribute money towards the compensation of their unsuccessful competitors[1] and would guarantee them certain rights of re-entry. The same considerations were fortified, in the case of the co-operative societies, by the fear of any form of organized action by distributors unless special recognition were given to the principle of mutual trading on which their business is based. But even the numerical majority of individual traders gave an unfavourable reception to the proposals for concentration. As a result they were quietly buried. We can presumably deduce from this experience that planned contraction of the distributive trades is not practical politics.

On the other hand, the suggestion that the distributive trades are over expanded is met by the counter-suggestion by the industry that it should, itself, organize limitation of entry by licensing. Trade Association policy has, in certain instances, had this end in view. This would be dangerous indeed, giving rise as it would to conditions of monopoly without any guarantee that the industry would be run in the public interest.

Public opinion in Britain is not disposed to admit the need for economy. Nevertheless, the people of the United Kingdom are in the position of a family which has certain things it wants to do: repair the house, buy more food and more clothes for the family and, perhaps, a car too. Its income (what it earns) is insufficient to buy all these things. Its choice is either to refrain from buying them until it has either worked harder and therefore earned more or has saved up to buy them; or the only remaining possibility is to borrow from the people next door.

The British chose the latter course during the war under the pressure of necessity to finance the United Nations' victory from the people next door. The serious problem is that the people of the United Kingdom are still, continuously, borrowing from abroad to finance their standard of living. The question is, whether a nation, which is still running progres-

[1]cf. Smith, *Retail Distribution.*

sively into debt,[1] can afford to spend such a large proportion of its productive power on the provision not of goods, but of services.

As a result of the removal of wartime restrictions on entry and of demobilization, the distributive trades are once more expanding.[2] In June, 1939, out of a total industrial population of 17,920,000, 2,887,000 (16 per cent of the total) were employed in distribution. By June, 1943, when full mobilization of labour had been secured, the total number of persons, employed in the distributive trades had been reduced to 2,009,000 (a reduction of 24 per cent). Thus, one in every four had removed to alternative employment. By the end of 1947, total employment was up to 2,351,000, having risen from 2,319,000 at the mid-year.

In the light of reasoned estimates of national need, it had been planned that total employment in the combined category. "Distribution and Consumer Services" should increase by 55,000 in 1947. The actual increase was as high as 136,000. Meantime, the drive for greater production and greater exports was held up by the lack of an adequate labour force in agriculture, coal and textiles and clothing.

The most disturbing aspect of the expansion is that it is taking place in circumstances that resemble those of the 1930s, except in so far as they have been exaggerated by wartime experience. The atmosphere is one of guaranteed margins, the maintenance of existing channels of trade and methods of distribution. One of the buttresses of the pre-war structure has, however, been removed. The authors of an addendum to the Second Report of the Retail Trade Committee point out that "the economy of these trades was based upon low wages . . . employers, who sought to pay decent wages to their employees were being persistently undercut by people, who did not care what conditions of labour they had for their staff so long as

[1]The deficit on western hemisphere account for the second half of 1948 was £140 million. This could not be offset by the surplus with other areas because of the non-convertibility of sterling. (*Economic Survey for* 1949, cmd. 7647)

[2]The Ministry of Food estimates, however, that the number of food shops decreased from 147,000 (1945) to 146,900 (1946). V. Appendix. This decrease indicates greater concentration of management.

they were cheaper than their competitors. . . . Until the National Joint Industrial Councils were established during 1941, there was no machinery for the general regulation of wages and working conditions. . . ." Trade Union demands for increased wages have been held in check during the war and post-war period by the government stabilization policy. But one factor in the pre-war situation which will not be retained indefinitely, is the availability of cheap labour to distributors.

Since the country cannot afford to pay more for distributive services without seriously endangering its recovery programme and since it is in urgent need of paying less, the issue seems to be clear: distribution must be made more efficient.

It has been the aim of this volume to show that the definition of the most efficient distributive techniques cannot be arrived at by the application of any simple formula like the relative operating costs of traders. It will always have, from the consumers' point of view, three distinct aspects. First, traders' margins, where they can be ascertained, provide evidence of operating efficiency; but it is evidence, which must be treated with caution, since differences in gross and net margins arise from a number of causes. Nevertheless, other things being equal, lower gross and net margins are preferable from the consumer's point of view. Other things are in practice rarely equal and have to be taken into account. It is necessary to determine, whether the lowness of a given trader's margins arises from long or short term causes. It would be a mistake to deduce that a certain type of trading unit was more efficient than another, because the trader was currently engaged in a price war and was therefore cutting his mark-ups as a purely temporary expedient. There is no doubt that sizeable reductions in operating costs are obtained by large-scale business, both at wholesale[1] and retail.[2] We cannot, however, deduce at once from this fact that large-scale trading methods should widely replace small-scale methods. There are two further important aspects of the problem from the consumer's point of view. The second main type of consideration relates to the wide variation

[1]See Appendix V.

[2]See Bellamy, *Oxford Institute of Statistics Bulletin* (October, 1946), "Size and Success in Retail Distribution," 324 ff.

in types of distributive service: some preferred by some shoppers, others by other shoppers. Differences in traders' operating costs result not only from differences in operating efficiency, but also from the provision of more and less expensive services. The third aspect is the character of the resources, that would be freed, if certain enterprises stopped. For example, if the cessation of certain business activities simply puts out of work people who are too old to change their jobs, or vacates premises which are useless for alternative production, then the cessation of those businesses is a net loss from the community's point of view. Finally, the difficulties of accurate social accounting must be met. For example, where the number of manufacturers and retailers is large the interposition of wholesaling as a separate economic function is likely to prove economical from the community's point of view. It will be difficult to identify the extent of these economies from the balance sheets of particular firms.

The discovery of long-term solutions must then await the collection of census data. But the time has come for the proscription by legislation of any business practices which impede the adoption of more efficient techniques and for the education of the public in the economics of distribution. Only a public, informed on the main issues involved, can appreciate the outstanding importance of distribution to the economic health of a nation, not only from the point of view of economizing resources in the distributive trades themselves, but in the contribution that efficient distribution can make to the production of the greatest quantities of goods and services that people want. It has been pointed out that the imperfect character of retail and wholesale markets, not hitherto fully appreciated, leads to a situation in which traders are not mirroring the preferences of consumers, but are demanding variety in their purchases as a competitive weapon; from the point of view of the final consumer, such variety is spurious and is, therefore, from the point of view of the nation as a whole, wasteful. It has been pointed out also that, owing again to the peculiar character of distributive markets, important influences have militated against the evolution of more efficient forms of organization and the adoption of more efficient techniques of purchase and sale and that the war has confirmed the protection afforded to vested interests.

Certain measures, tending to limit rather than to exaggerate the uneconomic forces, operating in an imperfectly competitive market, are immediately available. There is no need to wait to apply them. First consumer's information services[1] of some kind should be established with a view to assisting the final consumer to compare the serviceability, for example, of various brands of a commodity. Consumer's information on the availability of substitute articles in the market and the precise character of the variation in particular brands is pitifully inadequate.

The provision of information on the availability of competing consumer's goods was listed above as one of the primary services performed by distributors. It will remain so. But traders can, consciously or unconsciously, conceal knowledge of availabilities and the branding and advertising of articles can conceal instead of advertise the true character[2] of commodities from the buyer.

Secondly, all trade associations should be made to register with the appropriate government agency and to report their activities. A code of fair trade practices defining, among others, appropriate and economically justifiable means of securing stable prices should be constructed and made legally binding. Where price maintenance in any form is permitted, the dangers attending the fixing of resale prices by manufacturers and/or traders in agreement with one another and their consequent monopolistic character should be fully recognized.

It would be virtually impossible in practice and probably indefensible in theory to prevent the individual producer from maintaining the resale price of his own products. The danger of abuse arises when available substitutes are few and when traders are deprived of the possibility of stocking alternative substitute articles by the practice of boycott by associated producers. There are no strong economic forces in these circum-

[1]The United States Pharmacopoeia, for example, already provides such a service in the field of drugs.

[2]The Bayer Aspirin sells at $0.75 per ounce in the U.S. Its contents are $0.13 of acetylicylic acid : that is to say, the identical substance can be bought at a saving of 82.7 per cent.

stances guaranteeing the consumers interests. Such guarantees will have to be provided by law.[1]

Thirdly, research is required into consumers' preferences and the quantity and character of resources which would be freed by reducing the number of distributive outlets. Many managers of department stores hold that employees between the ages of 18 and 25 are from their point of view the most productive. If reduction in the number of employees in that age group would decrease the efficiency of this type of trading unit and if, on the other hand, it were found that the independent unit shop employed labour which would be relatively useless elsewhere, then the community would gain less by a restriction of the numbers of small units and an expansion of large-scale business than if this were not so. We need the facts. There is no point in limiting distributive services other than to free resources for production. It is known, for instance, that the proportion of old people employed in distribution[2] is higher than the national average. The older the labour the less mobile it becomes. We need to know, whether the older people are largely employed in certain types of trading unit and in certain commodity sectors before we can determine with any important meaning the quantity of resources engaged on distribution.

Legislation now, at last, provides the basis for a less negative interpretation of the principle of "restraint of trade." The Monopolies and Restrictive Practices (Enquiry and Control) Act, 1948 sets up a Monopoly Commission appointed by the Board of Trade. The Commission is to function separately from the Board of Trade, and decide its own procedure, but the Board of Trade retains the exclusive power to start investigation and the Commission may not even, without permission, proceed from an investigation of the facts to a statement of opinion, whether any harm is being done to the public interest. This seems an undesirable limitation but not necessary a fatal one. It is a strong point in favour of the measure that the Commission is to concern itself with restrictive practices even where there is no

[1]The United States National Recovery Administration refused to approve minimum prices unrelated to costs and opposed *uniform* cost floors for prices.

[2]See Appendix II.

monopoly, in the terms of the Act namely, "the existence of a single seller (or buyer) engrossing one-third or more of the market or the conduct of a trade (by number of participants) in such a manner as in any way to prevent or to restrict competition." Anything to do with wages or labour is, however, specifically excluded from enquiry by the Commision. The London *Economist* comment is appropriate—"At last somebody has done something about monopoly. That is a great gain. For something like a generation the initiative, both in discussion and in action, has been with those, who favoured monopoly and restriction of one sort or another—with what results are now bitterly apparent."[1]

No methods of control will be effective unless there is common agreement that the aim of control and of social policy is the more economic allocation of resources and the highest standard of living for all. The adoption of the Full Employment Policy should place this country in a favourable position to lead the way towards control in this field. While over-full employment with the attendant inflationary pressure has increased the pressure of the uneconomic forces detailed above, the maintenance of full employment should provide a suitable political atmosphere for the inauguration of remedial control measures.

It will, however, be found impossible to guard the living standards of those engaged or employed in distribution unless the over-expansion of facilities is reduced. Uneconomic duplication of retail facilities necessarily results either in higher marketing costs than would otherwise be necessary or in dangerously low wages or profits to many of those engaged in distribution—or to both. To those, who feel that we are still uncertain where to go, it should be emphasized that we cannot stand and are not standing still.

[1] *The Economist* (April 3, 1948), 356.

APPENDIX I

United Kingdom: Number of Shops, and Percentage of Sugar Registrations, 1940—1946

(*Grocers, provision merchants and general food shops*)
Analysis by type of shop

Number of Shops (Thousands)	1940	1941	1942	1943	1944	1945	1946
Total	191.4	157·8	153·8	150·5	147·9	147·0	146·9
Branches of multiples[1]	15·0	15·0	14·3	14·4	14·7	15·0	15·2
Branches of co-operatives	9·5	9·5	9·7	9·4	9·7	10·0	10·2
Independent retailers	166·9	133·3	129·8	126·7	123·5	122·0	121·5
Percentage of sugar registrations							
Total	100·0	100·0	100·0	100·0	100·0	100·0	100·0
Branches of multiples[1]	24·0	25·2	21·0	21·0	20·9	21·2	21·2
Branches of co-operatives	28·0	23·3	25·9	26·3	26·3	26·3	26·3
Independent retailers	48·0	51·5	53·1	52·7	52·8	52·5	52·5

Sources: Central Statistical Office, Annual Abstract of Statistics, No. 84, 1948

[1]Branches of a firm, other than a co-operative, with ten or more branches in the U.K.

APPENDIX II

United Kingdom: Estimated numbers of insured persons in the distributive trades in Great Britain at July, 1947[1]

Age group	*Males*	*Females*
14 and 15	55,000	90,000
16 and 17	63,000	126,000
18—20	23,000	150,000
21—25	101,000	137,000
26—30	119,000	69,000
31—35	127,000	60,000
36—40	125,000	62,000
41—45	102,000	58,000
46—50	67,000	46,000
51—55	58,000	31,000
56—60/59[2]	51,000	16,000
60—64	32,000	—

Source: Ministry of Labour and National Service

[1]No analysis of the numbers employed in the distributive trades is available for the pre-war period. The above analysis was made on the basis of a sample of 2 per cent of unemployment books exchanged in 1947. The figures relate to persons insured under the Unemployment Insurance Acts, and they therefore exclude (*a*) Employers and workers on their own account, (*b*) employees over insurable age (65 for men and 60 for women), and (*c*) non-manual employees earning more than £420 a year, who are not insured against unemployment.

[2]60 for men and 59 for women. Women cease to be insured on reaching the age of 60 and men on reaching the age of 65.

APPENDIX III

United States: Comparison of Operating Costs of Co-operative Retail Grocery Societies and Non-co-operative Grocery Independent and Chain Stores

Costs	Estimate for Co-op. Retail Societies		Independent Shops, Grocery, 1924	Chain Stores Grocery, 1929	
	Per cent		Per cent	Per cent	
Labour	8·10	8·50	10·90	8·90	10·30
Administration	0·40			1·40	
Rent	1·50		1·30	2·30	
Advertising	0·20		0·35	0·75	
Bad Debts	0·10		0·40	—	
Delivery	0·90		1·20	0·40	
Supplies, Maintenance, Depreciation	1·60		1·75	2·45	
Unallocated	—		1·00	1·25	
Total					
1 to 8	12·80		16·90	17·45	
Add interest	1·10		1·10	·75	
Total operating cost	13·90		18·00	18·20	

Source: Carr-Saunders, Florence and Peers, id., 375; quoted from Bulletins of the Harvard Bureau of Business Research.

APPENDIX IV

United Kingdom: Wartime Mortality of Retail Stores, Jan. 1940-*Dec.*, 1941

	(Classified by size of store) Leeds				Glasgow All shops
	Small single Branch Per cent	Medium and small Per cent	Large Per cent	All shops Per cent	Per cent
Non-food	(252) 32	(254) 18	(70) 13	(576) 24	19
Food A	(119) 20	(159) 9	(13) 0	(291) 13	10
Food B	(162) 19	(61) 2	(10) 10	(233) 14	12

(Figures shown in brackets denote the total number of shops in the sample).

Source: Oxford Institute of Statistics Bulletin (April 4, 1942), (Supplement 2) 3.

Note: The survey made in Leeds and Glasgow of the percentage of shops of various classes and sizes closed from January, 1940, until December, 1941, shows that, for all categories of shops, the rate of mortality of the small single branch shop was highest. The non-food category includes clothes, newsagents, jewellers, household goods, coal dealers.

Food A includes grocers, butchers, bakers, fruiterers, dairies, fishmongers

Food B includes tobacconists, confectioners, general shops, cafés. . .

APPENDIX V

United States: Wholesale Merchants and Industrial Distributors. Number of Establishments, Sales and Total Operating Expenses, by Business Size Groups, 1939

Business size groups (Size based on 1939 sales)	No. of establish- ments	Net sales	Total operating expenses	
			Amount	Per cent of sales
		$	$	
United States Total	92,794	19,418,547,000	2,662,646,000	13·7
$				
2,000,000 and over	1,102	5,025,212,000	445,878,000	8·9
1,000,000—1,999,999	2,052	2,792,112,000	344,558,000	12·3
500,000— 999,999	5,047	3,482,371,000	470,112,000	13·5
300,000— 499,999	6,195	2,376,989,000	353,329,000	14·9
200,000— 299,999	6,717	1,614,459,000	264,246,000	16·1
100,000— 199,999	14,226	2,017,339,000	361,367,000	17·9
50,000— 99,999	16,971	1,213,777,000	234,397,000	19·3
Under $50,000	40,484	869,288,000	188,759,000	21·7

Source: U.S. Government, *Census of Business* (1940), 20, Table M.

Note: From the above table it is clear that, *in general,* operating expenses in relation to the value of sales, decrease as the value of sales increase. The Census draws attention to the fact that this generalization is based on overall figures and does not apply to all kinds of business. For instance, in the tobacco trade, firms with 1939 sales between $500,000 and $999,999 showed the lowest expense ratio, while in the case of oil supply houses, those with 1939 sales between $300,000 and $499,999 showed the lowest expense ratio. Out of a total of 155 types of business, the expense ratio seemed to be indifferent to size and for 18 types of business the lowest expense ratio was found in the medium size brackets. The principal economies of large-scale appeared in the category of selling costs, consisting for the most part of salesmen's (travellers') salaries and advertising; economies of large-scale were also found in delivery charges and occupancy expenses. Warehousing and miscellaneous expenses remained fairly constant for all sizes of firm.

The following Working Party Reports have been issued to date by H.M. Stationery Office: *Cotton*, London, 1946; *Jewellery and Silverware*, London, 1946; *Heavy Clothing*, London, 1947; *Hosiery*, London, 1946; *Boots and Shoes*, London, 1946; *Furniture*, London, 1946; *Pottery*, London, 1946; *Cutlery*, London, 1947; *Wool*, London, 1947; Handblown Domestic Glassware, 1947; *Lace*, London, 1947; *Light Clothing*, London, 1947; *Linoleum and Felt Base*, London, 1946; *Rubber Proofed Clothing*, London, 1947.

A SHORT READING LIST

As introductory to economics generally:

1. P. A. SAMUELSON, *Economics: an Introductory Analysis*, McGraw Hill, 1948.

2. J. R. HICKS, *The Social Framework*, Oxford University Press, 1942.

And for a more advanced treatment of the economics of distribution:

3. E. H. Chamberlin, The *Theory of Monopolistic Competition*, Harvard University Press, 1932.

4. K. E. Boulding, *Economic Analysis*, Harper, 1941.

On Retail Trading:

1. H. SMITH, *Retail Distribution*, Oxford University Press, (2nd Edition, 1948).

2. H. LEVY, The *Shops of Britain*, Kegan Paul, 1947.

3. H. LEVY, *Retail Trade Associations*, Kegan Paul (2nd Edition), 1944.

4. U.S. Temporary National Economic Committee, Monograph No. 18, *Trade Association Survey*.

5. CARR-SAUNDERS, Florence and Peers, *Consumers' Cooperation in Great Britain*, Allen and Unwin, (3rd Edition), 1942.

On Wholesale Trading:

1. Braithwaite and Dobbs, *The Distribution of Consumable Goods*, Routledge, 1932.

2. Clarke and Clarke, *Principles of Marketing*, Macmillan (New York), 1946.

On Advertising:

1. N. H. Borden, *The Economic Effects of Advertising*, Irwin, 1942.

2. F. P. BISHOP, *The Economics of Advertising*, Robert Hale, 1944.

For Statistics on Distributive Trading:

1. Employment, Retail Sales and Prices (United Kingdom):
   (*a*) Central Statistical Office. *Monthly Statistical Bulletin* (for current data).
   (*b*) Central Statistical Office, *Annual Abstract of Statistics, No.* 84, 1948 (for period 1935-46).
   (*c*) *Population Census*, 1931.

Employment, Retail Sales and Prices (United States):
   (*a*) *U.S. Sixteenth Census: Census of Business* (1940) (*for the years* 1929, 1935 and 1939).
   (*b*) *Report of the Federal Trade Commission on Distribution Methods and Costs*, U.S. Government Printing Office, 1946.

2. Advertising:
   (*a*) United Kingdom. Kaldor and Silverman, *A Statistical Analysis of Advertising Expenditure*, Cambridge University Press, 1948.
   (*b*) United States. *Report of the Federal Trade Commission on Distribution Methods and Costs*, 1946. (Part V, Advertising as a factor in Distribution.)

INDEX

INDEX